STARK

ABITUR-WISSEN ENGLISCH

Rainer Jacob

Landeskunde USA

STARK

ISBN: 3-89449-165-5

D-85318 Freising · Postfach 1852 · Tel. (0 81 61) 1790

Inhalt

Fortsetzung siehe nächste Seite

Autor: Rainer Jacob

Vorwort

Liebe Schülerinnen, liebe Schüler,

in den neuen Englisch-Lehrplänen ist sehr viel von „stofflicher Reduzierung" die Rede – und das besonders im Zusammenhang mit dem Themenbereich „Landeskunde". Leider bedeutet das für Sie aber nicht, dass nun weniger verlangt wird. Vielmehr erwartet man, dass Sie sich das nötige **landeskundliche Wissen** selbst aneignen. Dieser Band hilft Ihnen bei der **Vorbereitung Ihrer Klausuren und des Abiturs**, indem er die relevanten Kenntnisse kurz und prägnant vorstellt.

Landeskunde ist kein Selbstzweck und auch keine reine „Institutionenkunde". Land und Leute in den USA kann man erst begreifen, wenn man die **Wurzeln der amerikanischen Nation** kennt – die politische Konstellation, die Aufgabenteilung zwischen den Bundesstaaten und der Bundesregierung, die Rolle des *Supreme Court*, den Einfluss der Medien.

Dieses Buch ist in **allgemein verständlichem Englisch** verfasst, um Sie an das Niveau der mündlichen und schriftlichen Prüfungen zu gewöhnen. Jedes Kapitel ist in sich abgeschlossen und **sinnvoll untergliedert**, sodass Sie sich gezielt über abiturrelevante Aspekte der einzelnen Themenbereiche informieren können. **Zahlreiche Bilder** veranschaulichen die im Text erläuterten Fakten, **Schaubilder** stellen wichtige Zusammenhänge dar.

Ich wünsche Ihnen viel Erfolg bei Ihrer Vorbereitung und hoffe, dass Sie auch einige bisher unbekannte Seiten des „Landes der unbegrenzten Möglichkeiten" für sich entdecken.

Rainer Jacob

The Constitution of the United States

The constitution of a democratic country defines its political institutions and contains the basic laws upon which all other laws are founded. This description of the political system and the rights and duties of the citizens are usually assembled in a single document such as the German "**Grundgesetz**". Britain is an exception among modern democracies – it has no written constitution. This is so because England was the first country in which the principles of democracy and parliamentary government developed over the course of several hundred years. This process began in the 13th century when the English King John was forced to sign **Magna Carta**, which limited the powers of the Crown. With the passing of the **Bill of Rights** in 1689, which extended the powers of Parliament, the foundations of democratic institutions were finally laid. The British model of democracy had evolved and could from then on be developed and adapted even further by other countries. The advantage for the new democracies was that they could profit from the experiences gained in Britain and eventually work out an even fairer and more up-to-date system. This was the case in the United States where the **Founding Fathers** of the nation used the British system as their blueprint and improved it by including political theories of British and French philosophers of the Age of Enlightenment. Among these modern ideas which had never been worked out in practice in the Old World were: the separation of church and state, the sovereignty of the people, government by the people and effective checks and balances in government. Thus the United States became the first country in which these progressive concepts were transferred into political reality. However, this step forward did not come easily – self-determination was only achieved after a long struggle of the colonists in the New World against the reactionary forces of imperialism in the mother country Britain.

Historical Background

The battle for dominance on the American Continent between the two major powers England and France was decided in the **Seven Years' War (1756–1763)**. The result being that France lost her influence and Britain gained sole control of North America. Now that the French competition was eliminated a sensible and intelligent monarch was needed to handle the administration of the British colonies in North America. **George III** was crowned King of England in 1760, and, unfortunately, the incapability of the new sovereign soon became evident. Instead of granting the prospering colonies more freedom, the King and his advisors tried to exert more control and reduce self-government.

The interests of the colonists and those of the mother country soon collided. The first point of contention was the westward expansion of the colonies. More land for settlement was needed because the population was increasing fast. The British government, however, did not want to fulfil these demands because it feared that if settlers moved further west the Indian wars would erupt again. Therefore a **Royal Proclamation** was issued in 1763 prohibiting land conquest in the western territory between the Alleghenies, Florida, the Mississippi River and Quebec. This measure was totally ineffective, yet it contributed to a growing dissatisfaction on the side of the colonists with their mother country. The colonists felt neglected and exploited. They had the feeling that Britain was only interested in taking advantage of the colonies in order to increase her own economic position and prosperity. This impression was soon confirmed by the financial policy which the British adopted in the colonies.

A number of new laws were passed in London as the King needed more and more money to support the growing empire. The **Sugar Act** of 1764 put duties on molasses, wines, silks, coffee and a number of other luxury items and forbade the importation of foreign rum. Merchants in New England protested against the new tax because, they argued, the payments would ruin their business. The **Stamp Act** of 1765 increased taxes on newspapers and printed matter in the colonies. The tax laws caused serious tensions between the colonials and the British Parliament and culminated in the slogan "**no taxation without representation**". The colonists were no longer willing to pay taxes to their mother country without being properly represented in the House of Commons at Westminster, where the laws were passed. The colonists did not question the sovereignty of the King but they denied Parliament the right to pass laws without them being consulted first. The response of the British Parliament to this demand was the passage of the **Declaratory Act** (1766). It affirmed the authority of the British Parliament to make laws binding on the colonies – an insult for the colonists and at the same time an illustration of how unfeeling the parliamentarians in London were towards the maturing colony across the Atlantic.

American Revolution

In this atmosphere of growing tension two events happened in Boston which eventually sparked off the American Revolution. In 1770, British troops occupying Boston to enforce the new British taxes fired into a mob of about 60 rowdy Bostonians outside the Old State House. Five demonstrators were killed and eight wounded in the incident which became known as the **Boston Massacre**. Six years later, on December 16, 1776, 5,000 angry colonists gathered at the Old South Meeting House to protest against the monopoly of the East India Company and a tax on tea. Disguised as Mohawk Indians, American patriots threw 342 chests of tea from ships belonging to the East India Company into Boston Harbour. Angered by the **Boston Tea Party**, the British closed the port of Boston to trade until its citizens compensated the East India Company for the destroyed tea, and Parliament in Westminster passed a series of new laws, the **Coercive Acts**, to punish the colonists. In order to repeal these suppressive regulations, which the colonists called **Intolerable Acts,** representatives of twelve colonies (with the exception of Georgia) met in the **First Continental Congress** in Philadelphia. When on April 19, 1775, British troops tried to seize the arms of colonists at Lexington, Massachusetts, the first shot was fired. The **American Revolution**, the **War of Independence**, which was to last till 1783, had begun.

A clash between colonists and a squad of British troops became known as the Boston Massacre – an incident which eventually led to the Boston Tea Party in 1773 and the outbreak of the American War of Independence.

George Washington

On May 10, 1775, the **Second Continental Congress** assembled in Philadelphia and made George Washington commander of the American forces. The command was an honour, but Washington knew very well that it was a formidable task, too. He had to organize an army out of about 16,000 men, who were inexperienced in fighting and lacked military discipline. Baron von Steuben, a Prussian officer, joined the American forces and helped to drill and organize the troops. Out of necessity, Washington applied a new fighting technique. His men did not confront the enemy in formation, but attacked in small groups, spreading themselves all over the place. On July 4, 1776, the colonies declared their independence from Britain. In the winter of the same year Washington crossed the Delaware, captured the city of Trenton and took one thousand prisoners. The British soldiers – they were called **Redcoats** because of their uniform – fought back, but had great problems in trying to transport men and weapons because Washington's army frequently cut their supply lines. The tables turned when in May 1778, the French, Britain's old enemy from the **Seven Years' War**, came to the aid of the colonists. The British commander Lord Cornwallis surrendered his entire army on October 19, 1781, and two years later, in 1783, the final peace treaty, the **Treaty of Paris**, was signed. George Washington, the national hero of the new nation who had led the United States to victory over Great Britain, was elected president in 1789 and reelected in 1792. Both times he received every vote cast by the electors.

The Declaration of Independence

The **Declaration of Independence** was written in 1776, and adopted by the American Congress in Philadelphia on July 4 of the same year. Since then the 4th of July has been celebrated as **Independence Day** in the United States. When the Declaration was signed, a bell was rung, the **Liberty Bell**, which has become one of the most famous symbols of American independence. It was cast in England, in 1752, originally to commemorate Pennsylvania's **Charter of Privileges**. When the bell reached America, it was cracked and had to be recast. Until 1835, when it cracked again, it was rung every July 4th. In 1976, to mark the Bicentenary of the Declaration of Independence, Queen Elizabeth presented a new bell to the people of the USA. Engraved on this new bell, which came from the same foundry as the Liberty Bell, are the words "Let Freedom Ring". These words are taken from a hymn, and were used on August 28, 1963 by Civil Rights leader Martin Luther King in his speech "I have a dream".

Historical Background

In 1776, the 13 colonies were still at war with Britain, many people believed that a solution to the problems between the colonists and the mother country England would eventually be found. Only a minority believed in complete independence. But as anger towards the British grew, Congress decided that all links with the mother country should be cut. Five of the members of Congress were asked to write a formal Declaration of Independence. Among them was Thomas Jefferson (1743–1826), a representative of the state of Virginia, who later became the nation's third President (1800–1809). He wrote the first draft of the original document, working at his desk in the home of a young German bricklayer, Jacob Graff. Jefferson finished his work in two weeks, Benjamin Franklin and John Adams later made some minor changes.

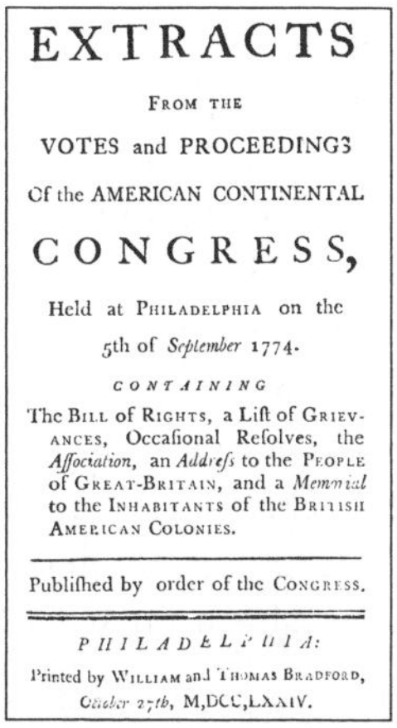

EXTRACTS

FROM THE

VOTES and PROCEEDINGS

Of the AMERICAN CONTINENTAL

CONGRESS,

Held at PHILADELPHIA on the 5th of *September* 1774.

CONTAINING

The BILL of RIGHTS, a Lift of GRIEVANCES, Occafional Refolves, the *Affociation*, an *Addrefs* to the PEOPLE of GREAT-BRITAIN, and a *Memorial* to the INHABITANTS of the BRITISH AMERICAN COLONIES.

Publifhed by order of the CONGRESS.

PHILADELPHIA:

Printed by WILLIAM and THOMAS BRADFORD, *October 27th*, M,DCC,LXXIV.

From 1774 to 1789 delegates of the North-American colonies voiced their complaints against the English crown at several meetings. The first of these congresses was held in Philadelphia in 1774. Among the representatives assembled were George Washington (picture on the right) and John Adams. In 1775 Benjamin Franklin and Thomas Jefferson (picture on the left) joined the delegates.

Equality and Human Rights

The Declaration of Independence begins with an indirect attack on the English King for his tyrannical rule. The colonists derive their right to resistance from the monarch's unfair administration. They hold George III responsible for the revolution and justify their rebellion. In the second sentence Thomas Jefferson and his co-authors express two revolutionary concepts, which have made the Declaration of Independence so influential, the ideas of **equality** and **natural rights**. Jefferson proclaims that "all men are created equal", which means that birth and position are irrelevant when we judge a person's value. It is not important whether somebody is born into a royal family or into a poor peasant's household. What is more, not only are all people equal, each individual also enjoys certain rights, which nobody can take away from him. These are rights which all men have, because they are human beings. This is why these rights are called **human rights**. They include the right of life, liberty and the pursuit of happiness. Even an unborn child has the right of life. An important point of view when one debates the question of whether abortion should be allowed. The right of liberty means that nobody can be imprisoned or sentenced to death without a fair trial. Everybody has the right to choose his own way of life, to decide where he wants to live, what he is going to do with his life – to be happy. This idea of the "pursuit of happiness" is the basis of the individualism of the American people, their firm belief in everybody's right – and choice – to decide for himself where his happiness lies.

Thomas Jefferson was not the author of this theory. The concept of natural rights was worked out in the 17th and 18th centuries when French, German and English writers (René Descartes, Gottfried Leibniz, Francis Bacon) questioned political absolutism, the unlimited, centralized authority in the hands of a monarch. The most notorious example being the French King Louis XIV, who said, «L'état, c'est moi» ("I am the state"). Thomas Jefferson used the writings of the most important natural-law theorist of the 18th century, the English philosopher John Locke (1632–1704), to phrase the Declaration of Independence. The great achievement of the American colonists lies in the fact that they, for the first time in modern history, used the most advanced philosophical theories to establish a new nation.

The Sovereignty of the People and the Role of Government

The Declaration of Independence clearly states the relation between a government and the people. All power lies with the people („Alle Macht geht vom Volk aus."), and the only function of any government is to make sure that the people can exercise their natural rights. This means the government must provide the framework within which each individual can lead his own life according to his/her personal wishes and aspirations. If a government fails in this role, if it abuses its power, the people have the right to overthrow the government. Here again, the main source which Jefferson used were the writings of John Locke. In his **Treatises of Government** (1690) Locke had written a justification of the **Glorious Revolution** in England and denied the king the divine right to govern. He expanded the 'contract theory' of government, the main argument of which was that all "just" governments were founded on consent and their only task was to protect people in their natural rights to life, liberty, and property.

Jefferson's words about the role of a government are still very much alive in American politics today. In his first **Inaugural Address** of 1983 US President Ronald Reagan of the Republican Party stressed the fact that Americans had always believed in government "of the people, by the people and for the people". Consequently, men do not owe their allegiance to a government or its leaders. For Jefferson, dissent was not only a right but also a necessity. "I hold that a little rebellion now and then is a good thing", he said.

Theory and Reality

The belief that all people are equal and each individual enjoys the same rights, in short, the dream of an open society without class barriers, has often remained an unfulfilled ideal because of people's inability to overcome their selfishness and rivalries. In George Orwell's fable and political satire *Animal Farm* the animals free themselves from the owner of the farm, Mr Jones, who has exploited them for years. They start their new ideal state on the farm based on the Commandments of Animalism. The first commandment being "All animals are equal". However, in the course of events, this ideal is being corrupted because some animals, the pigs, want to have more rights than the others. Therefore they change the first commandment with an amendment: "All animals are equal – but some are more equal than others." Through his experiences of communism and the history of the Russian Revolution the author of the fable, George Orwell (1903–1950), had become rather pessimistic about the possibilities of transferring the theory of "equality for all" into practical politics. He was convinced that people were corrupt and that they would betray the ideals of any revolution in the end. After changing the first commandment the pigs in *Animal Farm* establish their totalitarian and cruel dictatorship over the other animals.

The notion expressed by the Founding Fathers that America is the country which offers freedom and equality to all is one of the basic convictions upon which America's pride is founded. It is an ideal which Americans have cherished until today – although there has always been a difference between theory and reality. Even in the days when the Declaration of Independence was signed this ideal state of equality did not exist because black people were not included. All 56 of the signatories were white males of European descent, most of them wealthy property holders who owned black slaves – as did Thomas Jefferson. 267 slaves worked on his large plantation in Virginia. Nevertheless, in 1963 Martin Luther King referred to the Declaration of Inde-

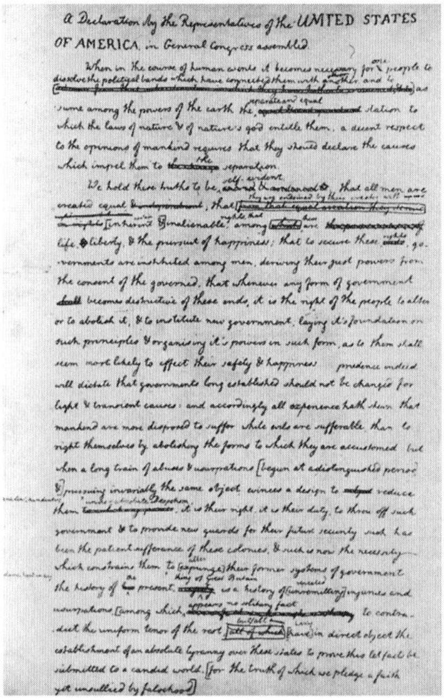
A Declaration by the Representatives of the UNITED STATES OF AMERICA, in General Congress assembled.

When in the course of human events it becomes necessary for one people to dissolve the political bands which have connected them with another, and to assume among the powers of the earth the separate and equal station to which the laws of nature & of nature's god entitle them, a decent respect to the opinions of mankind requires that they should declare the causes which impel them to the separation.

We hold these truths to be self-evident, that all men are created equal, that they are endowed by their creator with [inherent &] inalienable rights, that among these are life, liberty, & the pursuit of happiness; that to secure these rights, governments are instituted among men, deriving their just powers from the consent of the governed; that whenever any form of government becomes destructive of these ends, it is the right of the people to alter or to abolish it, & to institute new government, laying it's foundation on such principles & organising it's powers in such form, as to them shall seem most likely to effect their safety & happiness. prudence indeed will dictate that governments long established should not be changed for light & transient causes: and accordingly all experience hath shewn that mankind are more disposed to suffer while evils are sufferable, than to right themselves by abolishing the forms to which they are accustomed. but when a long train of abuses & usurpations [begun at a distinguished period &]pursuing invariably the same object, evinces a design to reduce them under absolute Despotism, it is their right, it is their duty, to throw off such government & to provide new guards for their future security. such has been the patient sufferance of these colonies; & such is now the necessity which constrains them to [expunge] their former systems of government. the history of the present king of Great Britain is a history of [unremitting] injuries and usurpations, [among which, appears no solitary fact to contradict the uniform tenor of the rest, but all have] in direct object the establishment of an absolute tyranny over these states. to prove this, let facts be submitted to a candid world. [for the truth of which we pledge a faith yet unsullied by falsehood]

The "Original Rough Draught" of the Declaration of Independence was written by Thomas Jefferson in June 1776. Later changes were added by John Adams and Benjamin Franklin.

pendence when he told the masses about his dream of a united and free America.

Today equality still seems a long way off in the United States for the disadvantaged, the working poor and other social groups which are confronted with discrimination on the grounds of their race, sex or age. For them the American dream of freedom and opportunities for all is still a dream, something which they find hard or even impossible to fulfil. Wealth in the US is still distributed unequally and there are large minority groups – such as the African-Americans, Native Americans, and Hispanics – who do not at all participate in the prosperity of the country but live on the fringe of the American society. In his second Inaugural Address in 1997 President Clinton asked his countrymen to help these groups "and treat all its citizens as equals before the law and in the heart." Only then will the promise of the American Dream – the pursuit of happiness – become reality in the 21st century.

The Importance of the Declaration

Apart from its immediate purpose to provide a legitimation of the American Revolution the Declaration is a remarkable document because it proclaimed the principles of human rights and defined the **role of government**. Because of the clarity and the determination with which these new ideas were expressed the document has been regarded as the "first declaration of human rights" and it has become the "cornerstone of modern democracies". In 1789, during the French Revolution, the National Assembly of France adopted the **Declaration of the Rights of Man and of the Citizen**, which echoes the principles expressed in Jefferson's document. In the late 18th and the 19th centuries the concept of human rights as expressed in the Declaration of Independence was further advanced. In the 19th century, various peoples of Europe and of Latin America worked out their political systems by incorporating the ideas formulated by Thomas Jefferson. Germany's Grundgesetz (1949), which was elaborated after the end of World War II when the horrors of the Third Reich were still very much alive, owes a great deal to that Declaration passed by the American colonists in 1776.

Today there is general agreement that all human beings are entitled to some basic rights and that the observance of human rights is the most important feature of a democratic state. In the charter establishing the United Nations, all members were pledged to achieve "universal respect for, and observance of, human rights," The UN has continued to affirm its commitment to human rights, particularly in such documents as the **Universal Declaration of Human Rights** (1948). Today the original document of the Declaration of Independence is on view at the National Archives Building in Washington, D.C.

The Constitution

Historical Background

The **War of Independence** ended in 1783 with the victory of the colonists over their former mother country England. The Americans now faced the long and exhausting task of building their own independent nation. In 1777, while still at war with the British, the Americans had adopted their first constitution, the **Articles of Confederation**, which were ratified in 1781. This first constitution replaced an informal union of the thirteen states with a central, but very weak, government. It soon became evident that the system did not work, because it left too much sovereignty to the states. On the economic side for example, the central government had no authority to control trade and remove commercial barriers between the states so that in the end all states suffered financially. In international politics America's voice was not listened to because of the lack of unity among the states. At home **Shays's Rebellion**, an armed outbreak by debtor farmers in western Massachusetts in 1786–1787, and unrest on the Western frontier increased fears that the union would not survive. In 1787 Alexander Hamilton (representative of New York) and George Washington (representative of Virginia) managed to persuade the 13 states to send representatives to meet in Philadelphia to discuss the problems and decide on a new form of government. The legislatures sent their best men, among them James Madison from Virginia and Benjamin Franklin from Pennsylvania. Rhode Island was not represented and the only important men missing were Thomas Jefferson and John Adams, who held diplomatic posts, representing the United States abroad. George Washington was elected president of the meeting which became known as the **Constitutional Convention** and lasted till September 17. The politicians assembled in a building which was then the State House of the Province of Pennsylvania and is today known as **Independence Hall**, the same building in which the Declaration of Independence had been adopted nine years earlier.

The Framing of the Constitution

The enormous challenge for the representatives assembled in Philadelphia was to create a constitution which would hold the large and diverse nation together and, at the same time, protect the rights of the people. There were two opposing views as to how the union could be governed efficiently and also how the government could be controlled. One group, the **Federalists,** advocated the establishment of a powerful government, whereas the other party, the **anti-Federalists,** believed in leaving most power and responsibilities in the hands of the individual states. They looked upon a strong central agency with suspicion. As both sides presented good arguments for their convictions, it was clear that only a compromise could bridge the differences of opinion. James Madison from Virginia became the principal architect of the Constitution. Convinced that the prosperity of the country depended on a strong union he favoured a strong central government and presented his plan according to which the government was to consist of three branches – executive, judiciary, and legislative. This **Virginia Plan** did not appeal to the anti-Federalists because they felt too much power was being conferred to the central government. In order to dispel the doubts of the anti-Federalists a new solution had to be found. The problem was solved by Connecticut delegates Sherman and Ellsworth, who presented their **Great Compromise** in which Madison's suggestions were supplemented with the creation of a legislature composed of two houses: the Senate and the House of Representatives. The plan provided for equal voting in the Senate and proportional representation in the House of Representatives. This explains why Congress today comprises 100 members in the Senate – two from each state, irrespective of size and population – and of a varying number of members according to state populations in the House of Representatives. After prolonged debates and discussions the new plan was accepted and the Constitution was eventually drafted in September 1787. It was agreed that the supreme law of the land should be binding on all states and therefore had to be ratified by 9 of the 13 states before it could become law. In some states, particularly in Virginia and New York, there was still strong opposition led by the most prominent anti-Federalist Patrick Henry. It was mainly because of the forceful rhetoric of James Madison and Alexander Hamilton that the wavering states could in the end be convinced to agree to the compromise. The Constitution was ratified in 1788 and put into effect in 1789.

Preamble and Seven Articles

The representatives at the convention did not try to cover every possible eventuality, they preferred the Constitution of the United States to be short. It is composed of a Preamble, seven articles, and twenty-six amendments. An amendment is a change of or addition to the Constitution. The preamble states the reasons for adopting a constitution. Article I deals with the powers of Congress, the composition of the House and Senate and election to them, and restrictions upon the powers of the states. Article II covers the presidency, including election and powers, while Article III outlines the powers and responsibilities of the judiciary. Article IV describes relations between states and the admission of new states. In Article V the authors laid down how amendments to the Constitution should be made because they realized that with the development of the new republic changes might be required. An amendment may be made by a two-thirds vote of both houses of Congress and ratification by three-fourths of the states. Article VI states the authority of the Constitution; and Article VII says that nine states will have to ratify the Constitution before it becomes effective.

The Bill of Rights

When the Constitution was written, several states claimed it did not clearly guarantee the rights and freedoms that had been fought for in the American Revolution. In their eyes the Constitution merely provided rules for the machinery of government. Consequently, they refused to sign the document unless a number of amendments to the Constitution were added to provide more protection for individuals. These first ten amendments became known as the **Bill of Rights**, and they are a summary of the most important rights held by all US citizens. Canada has a similar summary, called the **Charter of Rights and Freedoms**. The Bill of Rights, which was passed by Congress in 1789 and became law in 1791, limits the authority of the government and guarantees the fundamental rights of all citizens. It is important to note that there is a difference between *human rights* and *civil rights*. Every human being enjoys human rights, even an unborn child, this belief was clearly expressed in the Declaration of Independence. However, not all people living in a country have civil rights, such as the right to vote, the freedom of speech, of press and of religion – the reason being that they are inhabitants of a country but not citizens, perhaps they are foreigners or below the age of majority, or serving sentences in prison. The Bill of Rights has been called "**the real bulwark**" of

American personal liberties. All over the world, from Europe to South Africa, countries have worked out their democratic systems using the Bill of Rights as the example to follow. The respect for civil rights – as well as human rights – has become a crucial test for any governments' legitimacy. There are also critical voices who argue that Americans insist on their constitutional rights too readily. Should their expectations not be fulfilled many US citizens believe that their rights are being violated. These Americans do not care for the good of the whole society, for public welfare, they are only interested in securing their own rights. John F. Kennedy referred to this self-centredness, when he told the nation in 1961: "And so, my fellow Americans: ask not what your country can do for you – ask what you can do for your country."

The **First Amendment** of the Constitution of the United States guarantees freedom of religion, speech, press, and assembly. The **Second** secures the right to bear arms: "A well-regulated militia being necessary to the security of a free state, the right of the people to keep and bear arms shall not be infringed." This amendment is used by American gun owners organized in the National Rifle Association to prevent stricter gun control laws, they call the Second Amendment their "Second Amendment birthright". The **Third** Amendment protects citizens against soldiers being quartered in private homes. The **Fourth** Amendment is the American equivalent to the British motto "Every man's house is his castle" because it protects people and their houses against unlawful entry, unreasonable search and seizure. The US Supreme Court has ruled since 1961 that evidence obtained by police by breaking into a suspect's home cannot be used in court. If the police do not have a warrant, for example, they are not allowed to enter a private house to look for evidence.

The **Fifth** Amendment concerns a person's right to remain silent in a court trial in order not to incriminate himself. This provision of the Bill of Rights was often referred to in the highly publicised O. J. Simpson trial, and it plays a major role in the popular novels of John Grisham. When cross-examined in court a defendant may "take the Fifth", which means he refuses to answer a question because his reply might be used against him. The US Supreme Court ruled in 1966 that a suspect has to be informed about his right not to say anything and to have a lawyer present if he so wishes.

Further Amendments

Since 1791 seventeen other amendments have been added, among them the so-called **Civil War Amendments** (Thirteen, 1861; Fourteen, 1868; Fifteen, 1870) which outlawed slavery, declared all people born or naturalized in the

United States to be citizens, and that the right to vote could not be denied because of colour. The **Fourteenth** Amendment of 1868 served as the legal basis in the fight for racial equality by the protestors of the Civil Rights Movement. The **Nineteenth** Amendment (1920) gave women the right to vote, the **Twenty-Second** Amendment (1961) extended the right to vote in presidential elections to residents of Washington in the District of Columbia. The voting age was lowered to 18 by the **Twenty-Sixth** Amendment (1971). The Founding Fathers put high obstacles in the path of passing new amendments, the latest number **Twenty-Seven** is about Congressional pay increases and was ratified in 1992.

Early in the year 2000, great parts of the American public discussed the question whether the US national flag needed constitutional protection. Patriotic Americans deplored the desecration of the flag often printed on trivial articles such as T-shirts, jeans, and coffee mugs, and that it was shown freely in advertisements. They maintained that this disrespectful use was an insult to America's veterans and to the nation and called for an amendment to the Constitution to protect the flag. A first step was taken in the House of Representatives where a bill was passed to enable Congress to enact legislation. However, after heated discussions, the US Senate narrowly defeated the proposed constitutional amendment by a 63–37 vote, four short of the two-thirds majority needed. Many Senators argued that the flag, while a precious symbol, was above the need for such protection. The initiative failed.

The System of Government

Creating a Federal Government

In 1787 fifty-five delegates of the newly-founded "United States of America" met in Philadelphia to amend the "Articles of Confederation", a compact which the thirteen colonies had adopted in 1781. The bitter years of the **War of Independence** with their former mother country England had taught the colonists that the loose association which they had agreed upon in the "Articles" was too weak to manage the problems of the fledgling nation. Problems abroad and at home continued to grow. There was no uniform stable currency in the thirteen states, each printed its own money. Several states quarrelled over state boundaries. In Massachusetts a former Revolutionary War army captain, Daniel Shaw, led a rebellion of impoverished farmers. In short, it was a time of turmoil and chaos. Calls for a strong central government were supported by war hero George Washington, who warned: "There are combustibles in every state which a spark might set fire to." The main task of the Constitutional Convention, therefore, was to improve the **Articles of Confederation**. Very soon, however, this aim was abandoned and the delegates opted for a more comprehensive and radical solution. They worked out a completely new political system for the new-born nation instead, the basics of which they laid down in the **American Constitution**.

The Separation of Power

The framers of the Constitution achieved two aims: they created a federal government with far-reaching authority and secured the protection of the rights of individual people at the same time. The foundation of the system is the firm conviction that final authority is vested in the people – a belief which had already been expressed in the **Declaration of Independence**. The people do not exercise their authority directly, they delegate it to officials who carry out the day-to-day business of governing the nation. To avoid an excessive concentration of authority, as existed then in the monarchies in Europe, power was separated into three branches – the executive branch, the legislative branch and the judiciary branch. All three branches were equally important and each branch controlled the others. The system was effective enough to govern four million people in 13 different colonies along the Atlantic coast at the end of the eighteenth century. Today the same system, with only 27 amendments, serves the needs of more than 220 million people in 50 states from the Atlantic to the Pacific Ocean. This proves the strength and soundness of the framework conceived in Philadelphia in 1787 and makes the **American Constitution** the world's oldest written constitution in force. Moreover, countries all over the world have used it as the model to organize their democracies.

The Executive Branch

The Office of President

The delegates at the Constitutional Convention unanimously elected George Washington the first president, John Adams was voted vice-president. Both were sworn into office on April 30, 1789 in New York, which **Congress** had fixed as the seat of the new government. In 1800, the capital of the new republic was moved to Washington in the District of Columbia (D. C.). A stately grey sandstone building which was painted white, aptly named **White House**, has since been both residence and office of the president of the United States. The Constitution requires the president to be a native-born American citizen of at least 35 years of age who must have lived in the United States for at least 14 years. He is elected by the people through the **Electoral College** to a four-year term and can be re-elected once.

The White House, on Pennsylvania Avenue, Washington, D.C., is the official residence of the President of the United States.

The president's chief duty is to protect the Constitution and enforce the laws made by Congress, which means he has to sign the bills before they can become law. A look at the president's further functions makes his powerful position obvious. The president is **Head of the Executive** and also **Head of State**, he is the **commander-in-chief** of the country's armed forces and in times of emergency can give executive orders that do not have to be passed by Congress. He has overall responsibility for formulating and executing the foreign policy of the United States and participates in summit conferences where chiefs of state meet for direct consultation. All American presidents in the 20th century have actively been involved in world politics. President Woodrow Wilson headed the American delegation to the Paris conference at the end of World War I; President Franklin D. Roosevelt conferred with Allied leaders at sea, in Africa and in Asia during World War II. President Clinton played an important role as conciliator between Palestinians and Israelis in the Middle East conflict. The president appoints **Supreme Court** judges and ambassadors, and chooses the heads of all executive departments and agencies. The president also has the pardoning power to shorten prison terms or reduce fines of people who have been convicted of breaking the law. Because of the vast range of roles and responsibilities which a president holds some political analysts have spoken of the "imperial presidency", meaning the position is so powerful that it resembles that of a monarch of old times, especially when the office is in the hands of a strong personality such as Franklin D. Roosevelt. However, in the Constitution the Founding Fathers laid down one measure which can be used to remove the president from office, if he abuses his authority and fails in his duties.

Removing a President: Impeachment

The public demands that the man in the White House observes a higher moral standard than ordinary men and women. John Steinbeck characterised the very special relationship of the American people to their president like this: "We have established a tough but unwritten code of behaviour for him, and the slightest error causes a lot of exaggerated accusations. We subject him and his family to constant examination and accuse them for things that we ourselves do every day." In 1998 a storm broke loose over President Clinton's personal conduct. His opponents accused him of obstructing justice to cover up an affair he was supposed to have had with a young White House trainee and asked him to resign. Clinton refused and the opposition tried to remove the president from office on **impeachment** – a drastic measure provided for in Article II, Section 4 of the Constitution.

The impeachment process is a trial which goes through eight stages. Stage 1 is the **Resolution in the House of Representatives**, the final stage is the **Senate vote**, when the Senators vote on each article of impeachment. If a two-thirds majority supports impeachment, the president is removed from office. Since 1789 only seventeen people, thirteen of whom were judges, have been impeached. Seven were convicted by the **Senate**. Most impeachment resolutions that have been filed against presidents have died in the initial stages (in the **House Judiciary Committee**), only few went further. In 1843 President John Tyler was charged of corruption and misconduct. Tyler followed the impeachment process until stage 3, when the House rejected the charges. In 1868 the charge against President Andrew Johnson was serious misconduct. He followed the impeachment process until final stage 8, the Senate vote, where he was acquitted by a margin of one vote. Johnson completed his term. In 1974, following the **Watergate scandal**, the charge against President Richard M. Nixon was obstruction and abuse of power. Nixon followed the impeachment process up to stage 6, but resigned before the final vote was taken. The impeachment against President William Jefferson Clinton began in September 1998. The **independent counsel**, Kenneth W. Starr, sent a report to the House saying he had found "substantial and credible information" constituting grounds for impeachment of President Clinton. The charges were perjury and obstruction of justice. Clinton went through the whole trial and on February 12, 1999, was acquitted by the Senate. All these months the executive had been paralysed, because not only people in America but all over the whole world were waiting for the final outcome of the proceedings. What it showed in the end was that nobody, not even the most powerful man in the world, the US president, is above the law. If he really fails in his duties and in his conduct, he can be removed from office.

During his impeachment trial President Clinton appears in the Senate, presided over by Vice-President Gore and Republican Newt Gingrich.

The Departments and Agencies

Fourteen departments and a number of executive agencies, such as the **National Security Council**, the **Office of Management and Budget**, the **Council of Economic Advisers**, assist the president in the daily administration of the affairs of the country. The heads of the departments, chosen by the president and approved by the Senate, form a council of advisers generally known as the **president's Cabinet**. The most important departments are the **Department of State** which advises the president on foreign policy, the **Department of Defense**, which has its headquarter in the Pentagon, the "world's largest office building", the **Department of Agriculture**, which supervises agricultural production, and the **Department of Education**.

A special section of the **Department of Justice** has gained more importance today, it is the **Drug Enforcement Administration (DEA)**. It is concerned with the fight against mafia-like organizations involved in the growing, manufacture, or distribution of drugs in the United States and on international markets.

In order to keep the government and the economy working smoothly there are a number of so-called independent agencies which are not part of the executive departments. These agencies include the **Central Intelligence Agency (CIA)**, which collects and evaluates intelligence information and makes recommendations to the National Security Council. The **Environmental Protection Agency (EPA)**, founded in 1970, whose primary function is to control pollution in the air and water, and to deal with the problems of solid waste, pesticides, radiation and toxic substances. The **National Aeronautics And Space Administration (NASA)**, established in 1958 to run the US space programme, placed the first American satellites and astronauts in orbit, and launched the Apollo spacecraft that landed men on the moon in 1969. Today, NASA conducts research aboard earth-orbiting satellites and interplanetary probes and operates the US fleet of manned space shuttles. All these departments and agencies form the executive branch of the federal government – a large organisation employing several million people. The president is the head of the civilian government work force, but he appoints only about 3,000 of them. The vast majority are civil servants who work independently of the government of the day.

Presidential against Parliamentary Government

Time and again political scientists have argued for the transformation of the American system of presidential government into one resembling a parliamentary system as it is practised in Britain. The main differences between the two systems concern the relationship between the executive and the legislature. In Britain, the executive consists of several members: the **Prime Minister**, the leader of the majority party, and his **Cabinet**, who are chosen by, chosen from and remain members of the **House of Commons**. In the USA, there is a single executive, the president, who is elected by the voters for a fixed term and his office is separate from the legislature. In Britain, members of the executive are responsible to and can be removed by parliament whereas in the United States it is very difficult to remove the president from office. Another feature is that in Britain – and in Germany – the offices of **Head of State** and **Head of the Executive** are separate. The queen or president stay above party politics, they try to speak for and represent all the people. In the US, both offices are combined in the president who may claim to be acting for all the people when in fact his is acting as party leader. The advantage of the system of parliamentary government is that the executive can carry out its programmes rapidly, because it has a majority in parliament. The president's intentions can be delayed by Congress. The presidential system, on the other hand, provides stable government, Cabinet overthrows and unforeseen elections are unknown, which make effective government more likely.

The Legislative Branch

Congress, the legislature of the United States of America, is composed of two chambers, the **Senate** and the **House of Representatives**. The creation of this system is the result of the discussions at the **Constitutional Convention** in Philadelphia in 1787. The representatives of the larger states argued in favour of proportional representation in the nation's legislature – each state should have voting power according to its population. The smaller states, fearing domination by the larger ones, insisted on equal representation for all states. The issue was settled by the "Great Compromise", giving every state equal representation in one house of Congress, and proportional representation in the other. This is why today the Senate consists of 100 Senators, two from each state. Rhode Island, the smallest of the American states, has as many senators as Alaska, the biggest state. Senators rank very high socially, behind the president and vice-president. They must be at least 30 years of age and are elected directly by the people every six years. In order to guarantee continuity not all Senators are elected at the same time. Only one-third of the Senate stands for election every two years, so there will always be enough people with experience in the law-making process. The Senate is presided over by the **vice-president** of the USA. Altogether the House of Representatives is composed of 435 members. How many members each state may elect to the House is determined by the size of population. In the first House of Representatives one member represented 30,000 citizens, today one member represents about 530,000 people. Six states have only one representative, California has 45. To qualify for election to the House, candidates must be at least 25 years old. They serve a two-year term – theoretically a short term of office but in practice most of the members are re-elected several times.

The primary function of Congress is the enactment of laws. To make a new law, a bill is introduced by a member into one of the chambers. Each house of Congress has the power to introduce legislation on any subject except revenue bills, laws for raising money, which must originate in the House of Representatives. The president may not introduce a bill, he has to find friends who will do this for him. After presentation the bill is discussed and normally sent on to a committee for detailed examination. The Senate has 16 standing, which means permanent, **committees,** the House of Representatives 22. The members of the committees specialize in specific areas of legislation such as foreign affairs, defence, banking, commerce or agriculture. This is to say, members of Congress acquire special knowledge in one or two areas of policy and as experts advise their colleagues when a new bill which falls into their field of work is presented. When a committee has approved of a bill it is then sent to the floor for open debate. When the debate is ended, the members of the chamber vote either to approve the bill, defeat it, table it – which means setting it aside – or return it to the committee. If a bill is approved, it goes to the other chamber because all bills must be passed by both houses of Congress. Once it has been passed by both chambers, the president signs it and it becomes law. If a bill is vetoed (not signed) by the President it can still become law if it is passed a second time by a two-thirds vote of both houses. The same pattern of separate branches is found in state, county, township and city governments. Each state has a governor as chief executive. Governors often became presidential candidates and some moved on the vice-presidency or presidency, e.g. Ronald Reagan (was Governor of California), Bill Clinton (Arkansas), Al Gore (Tennessee) and George W. Bush Jr. (Texas).

Congress

Legislative Branch, two chambers

- can overrule presidential veto
- decides on federal budget
- can impeach and remove judges
- can change laws
- can initiate constitutional amendments
- must approve presidential appointments to Supreme Court

- 100 members
- 2 from each state
- elected for a 6-year-term
- one third elected every two years

- 435 members
- states with a high population have more Representatives
- elected for a two-year-term

The Judiciary Branch

Supreme Court

The Supreme Court of the United States was created by the **Judiciary Act** of 1789 and consists of justices who are appointed by the president with the advice and consent of the Senate. The number of justices varied in the past, but since 1869 has remained at nine, including a chief justice. In 1986, Wiliam H. Rehnquist, a conservative nominated by then President Reagan, became – and still is – the 16th **Chief Justice**. Justices are removable only by impeachment. The chief justice presides over all sessions and five judges constitute a **quorum** to hear a case. There must be a **majority vote** before a decision is made. If a tie exists, the previous decision is upheld. The Supreme Court is the court of last resort for people who believe that **lower courts** have failed them. The Supreme Court Justices have the option of whether or not they wish to hear a case. Out of the approximately 5,000 cases appealed each year to the **United States Supreme Court**, it actually hears between 100 and 125 of them. When there are arguments about the meaning of constitutional rights the Supreme Court acts as arbiter, it interprets the articles of the Constitution and decides the issue. The Supreme Court alone has the power to strike down Federal or state laws that it finds to be contrary to the United States Constitution. The court's rulings affects not only the two contesting parties, known as petitioner and respondent, but also the life of all Americans because the court's decision becomes part of the law of the land. In this sense, the Supreme Court is the guardian of civil liberties in America. The Supreme Court has heard several hundred cases since it was established, some of which had controversial effects on the country's political and social structure. These historic decisions are referred as "**landmark decisions**".

The entrance to the building of the Supreme Court in Washington is inscribed with the motto: "Equal justice under law."

Landmark Decisions

The Supreme Court has often shown its independence of government and Congress influence. While some of its decisions were conservative changes, many were quite radical and often openly criticized by the government. While some decisions did not endure, many shaped American government and the breadth of individual rights:

Marbury v. Madison (1803): This lawsuit is one of the earliest and most celebrated cases. It was fundamentally a legal battle between William Marbury, justice of the peace, and James Madison, secretary of state, about their appointments. What is more important is the fact that for the first time the Supreme Court asserted its authority to oversee the constitution and declare acts of Congress which violate the country's basic law as null and void.

Scott v. Sandford (1857): Towards the end of the 19th century the Court took a few very conservative decisions which obstructed racial integration. The first case concerned Dred Scott, a Missouri slave who had travelled to and worked in "free" states and territories. Scott claimed that he should be entitled to his freedom under the legal principle, "once free, always free". But the Court said blacks could not achieve US citizenship and therefore could not sue in federal courts. The ruling which was a disaster for the blacks in the South helped to precipitate the Civil War and made the creation of the so-called "Jim Crow Laws" possible.

Plessy v. Ferguson (1886): The Court established the "separate but equal" doctrine which permitted racial segregation of public facilities. New regulations, the "Jim Crow Laws", were passed by the state legislatures to establish racial segregation in buses, trains, restaurants, hotels, schools, theatres and even prisons. The "Jim Crow Laws" were used to maintain the unfair treatment and the limitation of the rights of the blacks. Although slavery was abolished the "separate but equal"-practices legitimized by the Plessy v. Ferguson ruling denied the black people in the South equal opportunities in employment and the right to vote.

After World War I the Supreme Court's conservative views met opposition from the liberalism of the **New Deal Era**. After some of his most important economic recovery programmes were invalidated by the court, President Franklin Roosevelt sought to reform the court by filling vacancies with more liberal justices. 70 years after the Plessy v. Ferguson decision the Supreme Court took a complete 180°-turn and outlawed "separate but equal" facilities because it had become evident that the ruling of 1886 had been used to oppress the African Americans. In 1954, the court issued its landmark desegregation decision and reversed its ruling of 1886.

7-year-old black child Linda Brown on her way to her local all-white elementary school in Kansas, accompanied by Civil Service agents.

Brown v. Board of Education of Topeka (1954): The case name refers to Oliver Brown, an African American, who appealed to the court when his seven-year-old daughter Linda was refused admission to an all-white elementary school in their hometown Topeka, Kansas. The Court ruled that racially separate school facilities in states was a violation of the equal protection clause of the 14th Amendment to the Constitution. The court concluded "that in the field of public education the doctrine of 'separate but equal' has no place. Separate educational facilities are inherently unequal." This decision eventually led to the prohibition of segregation not only in schools but also in jury service, marriage laws, and recreational facilities. The opinion spurred the **Civil Rights Movement** and provoked a fundamental change in race relations across America. The new liberalism of the Supreme Court continued through President Lyndon B. Johnson's administration when Chief Justice Earl Warren focussed the court's attention to civil rights and the enforcement of the **Bill of Rights**. In 1968, the Supreme Court ruled against racial discrimination in sales and rental of residential and other property.

Roe v. Wade (1973): The US Supreme Court ruled that states may not ban abortions in the first six months of pregnancy, arguing the 14th Amendment guaranteed a woman's right to end a pregnancy. With this decision, abortion was made legal nationwide. Although the ruling raised protests from a new "right to life"-movement, many US states liberalized their laws. A 1989 US Supreme Court decision defending Missouri abortion restrictions pleased opponents, but in 1992 the justices upheld the essential ruling of 1973.

The System of Checks and Balances

Looking at all the varied functions which the American president has, it may seem that his authority is unlimited. However, in the Constitution the Founding Fathers placed restrictions on the president to prevent a dictatorship. The other two branches of government, the Legislative (**Congress**) and the Judiciary (**Supreme Court**), were assigned responsibilities to control the Executive – and vice versa – so that a delicate system of mutual control developed in which the conflicting interests of the three groups were – and still are – solved by compromises. This elaborate form of government is called the **system of checks and balances**.

Here are a few example of how the system involves all three branches:

- Congress may impeach and remove the president for "high crimes and misdemeanours".
- Congress may override a presidential veto by a two-thirds majority in both chambers.

- Justices to the Supreme Court are appointed for life by the president, but the Senate must consent to this appointment (or refuse to confirm an appointee).
- The Supreme Court may declare acts of Congress unconstitutional, but Congress may propose an Amendment to the Constitution and thus help to change the Constitution.

Another factor operating as a "balance" is the system of **staggered elections**. The House of Representatives and one-third of the Senate are elected every two years. It often happens that if the president is a Democrat the people vote for a Republican Congress in the elections, and vice versa, which means that a president will have to contend with a majority from the other party in one or both of the two chambers of Congress. This happened to the Clinton administration, when the President, who was a Democrat, wanted to introduce a better health provision scheme. As the president is not a member of Congress, he can only propose a bill to be discussed in Congress. When he needs more money for his programmes or for military operations, he has to ask Congress for funds. Clinton's bill failed, because Congress, dominated by a Republican majority, discarded the president's proposals.

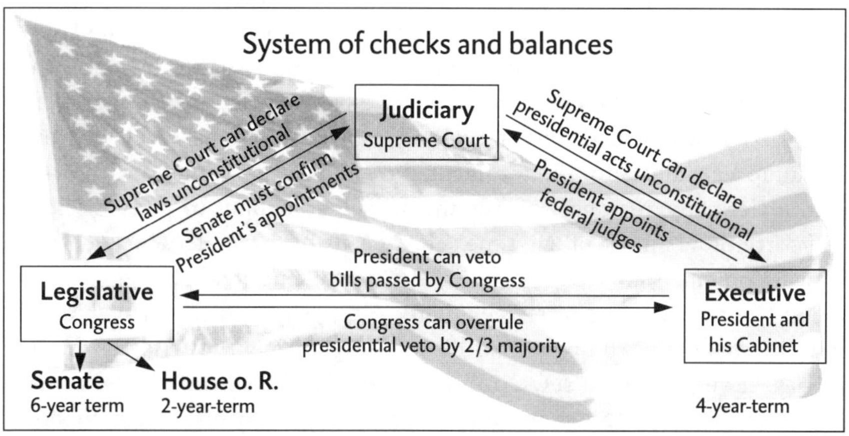

On the other hand, the President may veto laws passed by Congress. The result is that both can keep each other in check and a stalemate situation ('Patt-Situation') may occur. If Congress decides to be uncooperative, the president faces difficult times indeed because the president cannot govern against the majority in both chambers of Congress. He has to shape his policy to find a majority for his plans in Congress. When Ronald Reagan and George Bush, both of the Republican party, were presidents, they faced a majority of the opposing Democrats in both Senate and House of Representatives. This situation was described as "**deadlock**". In his Inaugural Address Republican George Bush appealed to the Democrat majority in Congress asking them to rise above party politics and cooperate with his administration. In difficult times all parties have to stand together united: "In crucial things, unity – and this, my friends, is crucial." (George Bush: Inaugural Address, January 20, 1989). When the Gulf War began in 1991, George Bush could rely on the undivided support of the American Congress. His son George W. Bush, elected in 2000, could count on a Republican majority in the House of Representatives.

Parties

There are two major political parties in the United States, the Democratic and the Republican. Although there are other minor political groups as well, usually referred to as "third parties" only the two big ones have played an important role on the national level. This two-party system has evolved over the years, and the presidency or Congress have either been in the hands of the Republicans or the Democrats. In contrast to Europe, parties in the United States are not tight ideological organisations bound together by some basic conviction, such as the belief in socialism, liberalism or conservatism. They are basically loose associations of local and state organisations which join forces to put up a candidate for the presidential elections every four years. In Britain and in Germany, members of parliament have to submit to party discipline and party orders most of the time. This means for example when there is a division members are told how to vote in parliament. If a member refuses to follow the party line too often, he might be "punished" by the party whip and lose the support of the party and his seat in parliament. Critics say that the parties "have parliament sewn up", and their members firmly under control. In the United States things are completely different. Senators and members of the House of Representatives have little to do with party discipline, they vote as individuals. They do not owe loyalty to party leaders, they owe loyalty to their local or state electorate and vote accordingly to what the majority of the people in their constituency wishes. The two parties that dominate American politics have a long tradition which dates back to the **Constitutional Convention** in Philadelphia. When they discussed the role and responsibilities of a central federal government, the delegates were divided into two groups, **Federalists** and **anti-Federalists**.

Democratic Party

The anti-Federalist group had reservations about a strong central government and favoured the autonomy of the states. Its foremost representative was Thomas Jefferson, the author of the **Virginia Bill of Rights**. When he founded the party, he called it "Republican", but his enemies called it "Democratic", a term which they used in the meaning of "demagogic". Born of the anti-Federalist movement, it was, until the beginning of the 20th century, the defender of the states against federal intervention. In this period, Democrats opposed a central bank and protective tariffs. This anti-Federalist tendency reversed itself completely when the Democrat F. D. Roosevelt was elected president (1932). Since then the Democrats have supported central intervention in state affairs. In 1960, Democratic candidate John F. Kennedy won the presidential election beginning the **New Frontier** era that stressed US world responsibilities for peace and economic growth at home. In 1984 the Democrats became the first major party to choose a woman (Geraldine Ferraro) for its vice-presidential candidate.

In the 19th century the party gathered its support mainly from farmers, small businessmen, and the professional classes. Today, Democrats win regularly in the South and in the cities of the north and east which have the largest foreign-born population, especially of Catholic and Jewish faith. The party also tends to attract votes from "outside" groups and, generally speaking, low-income and poor families. This view of the Democratic party as the supporter of the disadvantaged was mainly formed during the presidency of Franklin D. Roosevelt. Roosevelt was elected president in 1932 because the American people thought that President Herbert Hoover did not do enough to fight the **Depression**. Within days of taking office, Roosevelt proposed recovery and reform legislation to the US Congress, and soon the government was creating jobs for hundreds of thousands of people. Most of the programmes started during the Depression era were temporary relief measures, but one of the programmes – Social Security – has become an American institution. In the 1960s, the Democratic presidents J. F. Kennedy (the first Catholic president) and L. B. Johnson not only improved the civil rights legislation for the Afro-American population and America's native inhabitants, they also established better social assistance programmes. After Kennedy's assassination Lyndon Baines Johnson (1908–1973) became the 36th president of the United States (1963–1969). In his first State of the Union address, he presented an ambitious programme of domestic legislation to raise the quality of American life and eliminate poverty, calling for an "unconditional war on poverty".

The legislation passed by Congress in 1965 alleviated the lives of many underprivileged Americans. People living below the poverty line received foods stamps, certificates with which they could buy food. Cheaper accommodation became available for people with low incomes because the state financed the building of houses. Following Johnson's appeal two social plans, called **Medicaid** and **Medicare**, were elaborated to assist unemployed and elderly people in case of illness and these programmes are important pillars of social security in the United States today. Medicaid pays medical treatment for poor people, and at a cost of about $156 billion a year is today the nation's largest social-welfare programme. Medicare covers the medical bills of people who are over 65 or who are disabled. However, the new social security schemes of the Johnson administration did not eradicate poverty completely. When the Democrat Bill Clinton came into office in 1993, he tried to continue along Johnson's lines in view of the fact that there were still too many unemployed Americans who did not qualify for Medicare or Medicaid and who could not afford private health insurance. Assisting these uninsured Americans was one of Clinton's priorities. After widespread discussion and debate across the country Clinton's radical proposals were discarded by the Republican majority in Congress. However, in 1996 Congress passed legislation designed to make health insurance more available to working families and their children. A complete reform of the social security system to knit a tighter social safety net still remains on the agenda of the Democratic party. It is estimated that one in seven Americans is without health insurance.

Republican Party

The Republican Party, also known as the G.O.P., or **Grand Old Party**, was organized in 1854 as an amalgamation of Whigs with businessmen, workers, and professional people who formerly had called themselves Independent Democrats, Know-Nothings, Barnburners, and Abolitionists. John C. Fremont was the party's first presidential candidate in 1856. Its first successful candidate was Abraham Lincoln, elected in 1860. The party was particularly strong in the period from the Civil War to 1932. After 1932, Dwight Eisenhower (1952, 1956) and Richard Nixon (1968, 1972) each won election victories for the Republicans, but both had to work with largely Democratic Congresses.

Republican Ronald Reagan became president in 1980 and was re-elected in 1984.

Many Protestants and people of Teutonic origin are found in the ranks of the Republicans. By and large, the party supports the interests of manufacturing and commercial enterprises, and most of the middle class and the wealthy vote Republican. In 1980, Ronald Reagan, a former movie actor and governor of the state of California, won a landslide election to become the 40th president of the United States. In his **Inaugural Address** he outlined a new policy which was named "**Reaganomics**". He limited government spending and reduced government intervention in the private sector to leave more room for private initiative.

This attitude is a reflection of the traditional view of the American people that everybody should take care of himself. "**Self-reliance**" is the keyword and since the days of the pioneers and settlers this has always been regarded as a basic value in American society. Helping the poor had been in the hands of private charity organisations and welfare programmes and a social net comparable to European standards did not exist. Reagan's idea of "back to basics", which on the surface sounded good and sensible, turned into hard times for the sick, handicapped and elderly, because during Reagan's presidency social support programmes, which the Democrats had initiated earlier, were cut or even stopped altogether.

The Differences Between the Parties

It must not be supposed, however, that the Republicans represent the Right and the Democrats the Left, there is no such clear-cut difference. There are many rich people who cast their vote for the Democrats and just as many poor who vote for the Republicans. Most analysts would agree, however, that the Democratic party is more liberal and the Republican more conservative. Republicans tend to put more emphasis on private initiative, whereas Democrats believe that the government has an obligation to provide for the needy. Both parties have supporters among a wide section of the population and their political programmes and platforms reflect what the majority of the people think and want. Many Americans sided with Ronald Reagan's demand for a reduction of government spending on welfare programmes. By the 1980s, these programmes were consuming a substantial portion of the overall budget without producing the desired effect because in spite of increased spending the number of Americans in poverty was not decreasing. And so politicians in both parties were of the opinion that a reassessment of approaches was necessary. The idea of more effective government spending in the social area was taken up by President Clinton of the Democratic party in the 1990s.

Many people felt reminded of what Republican President Reagan had said 15 years earlier. This shows that the programmes of the parties are always "up-to-date" and designed to tackle topical issues, they are free from too much historic tradition or obligation and are not committed to an ideology.

Presidential Elections

The American Electoral System

A presidential election takes place every four years. According to the 22nd Amendment to the Constitution the President can be re-elected once. Candidates must be US-born citizens of at least 35 years of age, and they must have been residents of the USA for at least 14 years. More than a year before the actual election a large number of politicians announce their intention to run for the presidency – and a time-consuming and tiring campaign begins. In the past, when there were no jets or helicopters, no modern technologies of communication, aspirants to the office of President needed time to travel around in the country and make themselves known to the electorate. Today, however, things have changed and sceptics argue the campaign lasts much too long and costs too much money. The consequence is that only contenders with sufficient funds or wealthy friends can compete. In recent years millionaires such as Steve Forbes and Ross Perot took part in presidential election campaigns – without any real chances of winning the election – but they had the millions of dollars to pay for TV commercials and the whole propaganda apparatus to support their campaign.

Aspirants from the ranks of the two great parties, the Democrats and the Republicans, have to make great efforts to raise money from friends and supporters – if they themselves are not rolling in money. The worrying question then is how much influence will these wealthy contributors have on the future president? There are fears that the costly procedure of electing a US president is not at all democratic, because the "**fat cats**" (rich people who provide the money) have more influence than the ordinary voter. On the other hand, political analysts argue that the long campaign puts the candidates to a real test. They must prove how much stress they can stand and if they are physically and mentally fit for the most powerful and influential job in the country.

The American public saw John D. Rockefeller as a ruthless businessman whose Standard Oil trust had to be dissolved.

Stages of the US Presidential Elections

Primaries and Caucuses

The first hurdle in the race to the White House are the **primary elections.** For almost two hundred years the leaders of the Republican and Democratic parties picked their presidential candidates. They chose politicians with the best chances to win the election. In an effort to make this nominating process more democratic the first primaries were held in 1952. Over a period of months, from February to June in an election year, primary elections are carried out in an increasing number of states. The challengers of the incumbent president make themselves and their political policies known to as large a section of the public as possible. They criticize the president and his party and present themselves as the better alternative. The primary elections are not open to everybody – only party members can cast their vote because the parties want to find out who will be the most attractive candidate with the best chances in the general popular vote later in the year. The voters do not vote for a presidential candidate directly, they choose delegates to the national party conventions. However, voters know which presidential candidate a delegate will support. Another way to test voter sentiment and find the candidate with the most popular appeal, are the **caucuses.** These are informal local party meetings, where party members discuss the chances of individual applicants and express their preferences for a certain candidate.

The primaries serve as a testing ground for the parties and the independent candidates, and although the results are far from being conclusive, the results of one particular day often decides the fate of many aspirants. This special day is "**Super Tuesday**", a day in March, when primaries take place in a large number of important states such as California, New York, Ohio, Missouri and the New England states. It often happens that in view of the results of the primaries on Super Tuesday candidates with little perspective to secure a majority of delegate votes admit their defeat and withdraw from the race for the nomination.

National Party Conventions

After the primaries, in July or August of an election year, the national party conventions of the Republicans and Democrats are held in a city with a large number of Electoral Votes. Here the delegates of the parties nominate the candidate who will represent them at the election in November. These party meetings can best be described as lively spectacles which in many ways resemble the European 'carnival'. The convention hall is brightly decorated, bands play loud music and the state delegates wearing hats in their party and national colours cheer and applaud as prospective candidates are presented. Nominating speeches are delivered to win the support of the delegations assembled for a particular applicant. In the primaries the delegates had told the voters of their state whose nomination they would support. However, during the four days of the national party convention it may happen that the delegates have to vote for somebody else after all. This is the case when none of the candidates gains a majority on the first ballot, then the state delegations are no longer bound to their pledge. As soon as it becomes clear that one aspirant has secured a majority of all delegate votes the remaining votes go to him. This is called "**jumping on the bandwagon**" – to vote with the majority. In the end the party's candidate for the popular vote in November is supported by an overwhelming majority.

Once the nomination procedure is finished the candidate for the White House delivers an important speech, the **Nomination Acceptance Speech**. In it he addresses the delegates, the spectators in the hall and the whole American nation in front of their TV sets, summing up the goals of his campaign and his intentions if he is elected President. One of the most impressive Nomination Acceptance Speeches was held by John F. Kennedy in 1960 when he was nominated candidate for the **Democratic Party**.

Kennedy expressed his policy of the "New Frontier" by reminding the audience of the glorious past of the United States when the pioneers opened up the American continent, relying on their determination and team spirit: "Their motto was not 'every man for himself' – but 'all for the common cause'". Kennedy wanted to revive the pioneer spirit in the American people because he thought that unity and courage were as much needed now as they were in the 19th century: "… we stand today on the edge of a new frontier – the frontier of the 60's – a frontier of unknown opportunities and perils …". The 1960s were the time of the **Cold War,** and in Kennedy's view the greatest threat to the security of the American nation was the Communist Soviet Union. Social unrest at home in the wake of the Civil Rights Movement endangered the American nation. In order to meet these challenges it was necessary to close ranks and sacrifice personal goals for the common good. On the other hand, new technologies – space exploration – also opened up new horizons and opportunities. With this great speech Kennedy laid the foundation for his triumph over his rival Republican candidate Richard Nixon, who had served as Vice-President under the popular President Dwight D. Eisenhower. Kennedy's victory in the popular vote in November came as a big surprise because he was only 43 years old and he was a Catholic.

General Election

After their nomination the presidential candidates make every effort to win the votes of the uncommitted electorate. They present themselves at party rallies all over the country, appear on television and in chat shows, trying to appeal to voters of all ages and different backgrounds. The American election day is always the first Tuesday after the first Monday in November. This day was chosen as a compromise to please religious groups who were against Sunday, and business people who did not like Monday. Americans are eligible to vote from the age of 18, but they don't go to the polls in great numbers. Only about 50 per cent actually cast their votes, the majority watches TV as the results from the precincts (in Britain they are called constituencies) come in on the evening of election day. The American Electoral System is similar to the British system as far as it guarantees clear-cut majorities. Whenever a candidate gains the simple majority in a state, he is the winner, he "**carries the state**", even if he only had a majority of one vote in an electorate of three million. The votes for other candidates or parties are lost. The consequence of such a system, in which the "**winner takes it all**", is that smaller parties or independent candidates have almost no chances of winning, and that minorities are neglected. On the evening of election day the American public and the whole world know who will be the next president of the USA, although in the popular vote the American people do not vote for their President directly, they vote for delegates to the Electoral College.

Electoral College

The real Presidential election takes place in December when the members of the **Electoral College** meet in the 50 state capitals and the District of Columbia. The number of electors in each state is equal to its representation in **Congress**. To give an example, Kansas has seven members of the college, because it has two senators and five members in the House of Representatives. This constitutional body was devised when the Constitution was first written. The original idea behind the Electoral College was to have the President elected by unbiased people. But since then things have changed. Political parties developed and competed for power, and today party interests dominate the votes of the electors. Consequently, the meeting of the Electoral College has become a formality, and there is never much suspense about the outcome of the deliberations of the electors, because each state's electors are mandated by the popular vote cast in November, which means they have to vote in accordance with the results of the elections which took place in November. The candidate with 270 or more electoral votes is president, regardless of the popular vote.

Inauguration

The final step in the American electoral system is taken in January of the following year when the new President is sworn in by the **Chief Justice**, the highest judge of the **Supreme Court**. This is the oath of office he takes:

"I do solemnly swear (or affirm) that I will faithfully execute the office of president of the United States, and will to the best of my ability, preserve, protect and defend the Constitution of the United States." After this ceremony the new President makes a speech, the **Inaugural Address**, a keynote speech, in which he outlines his policy.

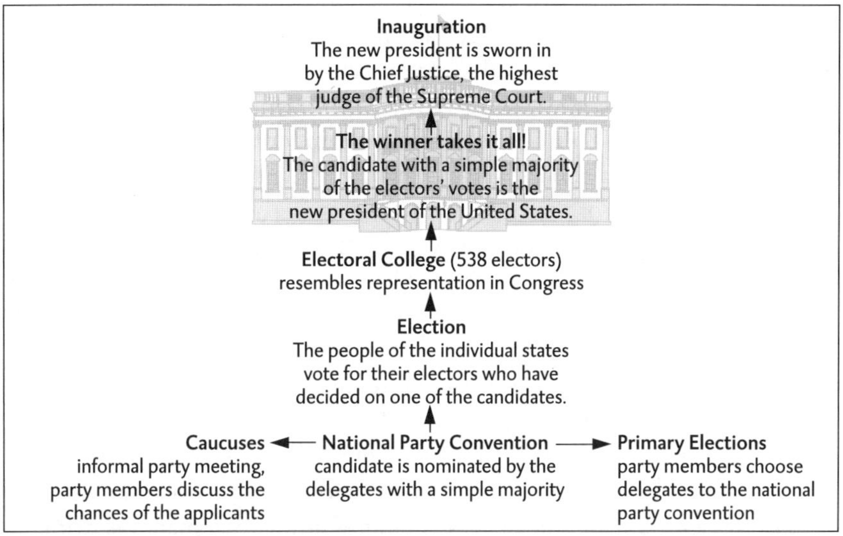

The Presidential Elections 2000

The presidential election of the year 2000 has gone down in history as one of the closest and most confused elections ever held in the USA. The turmoil and chaos of the whole process gave rise to criticism directed both at the candidates and, what is even more important, at the electoral system and the American democracy. The people of America cast their votes on November 7. Everyone across the nation and observers all over the world expected that, by the end of the day, it would be known who would be the 43rd president of the United States. This time, however, the result was less than clear and in the end it took 36 days before the struggle for the White House was finally over. Five weeks after the popular vote the candidate of the Democratic party, Vice-President Al Gore, gave up his fight to claim the presidency and admitted that he had lost the race, the technical term being that 'he conceded' to Republican candidate George W. Bush.

The Presidential Aspirants

The presidential election to determine the successor of the popular Democratic president William (Bill) Jefferson Clinton attracted the interest of the American nation and of people all over the world only after November 7, the day of the popular vote. Americans are not eager voters and, as usual, only about 50 per cent of those allowed to vote actually turned up at the polling booths. The extraordinary low turnout – compared to European or German standards where 70 or 80 per cent use their right to vote – was explained by the fact that people had lost interest during the long and tiresome election campaign, which traditionally lasts for more than a year. In addition, in 2000, neither the Republicans nor the Democrats had found an attractive candidate with popular appeal. The Democrats had no real choice, because Al Gore had served for eight years as Vice-president and nobody within the Democratic party was brave enough to stand against Mr Gore's decision to run for the presidency. The Republicans were able to choose, but not all party members were enthusiastic about the nomination of the right-wing Texan governor George W. Bush. So the election campaign got under way with both candidates trying to convince their followers and arouse the interest of the undecided voters. On the advice of his public relation and media managers – the so-called 'spin doctors' – Al Gore more than once changed his style, his clothes and his gestures because Americans regarded him as too stiff and reserved. He gained himself the nickname 'The Robot'. His contender, George W. Bush, son of former US President George Bush, was regarded as the representative of the rich white conservatives in America, a man of law and order, with no experience and little interest in foreign politics. Above all, his failures as a young man, his drinking and marriage problems, made the headlines during the campaign – and so most people expected Al Gore to win the presidency.

The Importance of the Electoral College

According to the American electoral system a presidential candidate must win the majority of the votes in the Electoral College, not necessarily the popular vote. The Electoral College officially appoints the president. This system was set up by the Founding Fathers and is the result of a compromise between the advocates of a direct vote by all citizens and others who wanted Congress to appoint the president. There are 538 members in the Electoral College – one for each member of the House of Representatives and the Senate, plus three electors from the District of Columbia. Each state has a certain number of electoral votes and the candidate who wins the simple majority in the popular vote gets all the electoral votes of this state.

This "winner-takes-all principle" seems unfair to a lot of people. Florida and its 25 electoral college votes proved to be the key to the 2000 election. Both, Gore and Bush, needed to win the sunshine state in order to have at least 270 votes in the Electoral College, the majority needed to become president. Although more than 6 million Americans went to vote on November 7 in Florida, only a mere 537 votes separated the two candidates, with Bush in the lead. As the result was so close the votes were counted again. When some irregularities were detected lawyers from both sides stepped in arguing for more recounts or trying to stop the process. The US Supreme Court eventually put an end to the chaos by ruling that the state-wide recount of votes ordered by the Florida Supreme Court was unconstitutional and therefore should stop. With this decision Republican George W. Bush and his vice presidential running mate, Dick Cheney, had won the Electoral College votes of 30 states, a total of 271 electoral votes. His Democratic opponent Al Gore and his running mate, Connecticut Senator Joseph Lieberman, had received 267 electoral votes. Al Gore accepted the decision of the judges and conceded the election on December 13, 2000. In his speech, he said he would "honour the new President-elect and do everything possible to help bring Americans together."

Frustration and Calls for Modernization

The arguing about counts and recounts, the alleged irregularities and the decision of the Supreme Court divided the nation and caused widespread anger and bitterness on both sides. Many of Mr Gore's supporters, in particular Afro-Americans and poorer people, were deeply disappointed and felt that they had been "robbed of victory", because they believed that if the hand recounts in Florida had been resumed they would have shown that Mr Gore had won the state. Even Republicans admitted that the punch card ballots in many Florida counties were susceptible to voter error. What further enraged Democratic voters was the fact that for the first time since 1888 the candidate who had lost the popular vote became president. George W. Bush received 300,000 fewer votes nationwide than Mr Gore. To calm down unhappy voters the new President-elect promised to try to heal the country's divisions. On December 13, 2000, in his speech to the American people Bush paid respect to Vice-president Al Gore and called for unity: "Our nation must rise above a house divided," he said. "Americans share hopes and goals and values far more important than any political disagreements. Republicans want the best for our nation. And so do Democrats. Our votes may differ, but not our hopes." Bush also explained his political plans for the country. He spoke about improving public schools, strengthening Social Security and Medicare and his promise to cut taxes.

1. President

Candidate	Popular Vote	Percent	Electoral Votes
George W. Bush (REP)	49,782,288	48	271
Albert Gore (DEM)	50,140,140	48.3	267
Patrick Buchanan (RFM)	449,041	0.4	0
Ralph Nader (GRN)	2771,871	2.7	0
Electoral votes needed to win: 270			

2. Senate and House of Representatives

	Republicans	Democrats	Independents
Senate	50	50	
House of Representatives	221	212	2
For the first time since 1880, the Senate is split down the middle.			

Election Results 2000

On January 20, 2001, George W. Bush was sworn in as the 43rd president of the United States. The **inauguration ceremony** in Washington ended one of the most disputed presidential elections in US history, but the debate about the American electoral system is not yet over. The presidential election of 2000 proved to the world that the Electoral College, the voting and counting process are outmoded. Broad discussions about major reforms of a system which was devised in the 18th century by white, slave-owning representatives of the affluent ruling upper class have begun. With its more than 200 years the US Constitution is older than the French, German, Italian, Belgian, Spanish and Greek constitutions. Political observers say that the American democratic system and the Constitution must be modernized if the nation wants keep on telling the rest of the world how a democracy should be run. Blatant inadequacies (the disregard of ethnic minorities) and unfair regulations (the composition of the Senate for example) must be abolished. Under the present system only millionaires with sufficient funds or wealthy friends can compete in a presidential race. Less affluent contenders stand no chance because they cannot afford the enormous costs of a campaign in our media and internet age. It is not surprising then that 'oil man' George W. Bush is one of the richest US Presidents ever.

Immigration

A Nation of Immigrants

The United States has been called “a nation of immigrants” because of its great ethnic diversity and the fact that only about 2 million people of its total population of about 270 million are descendants of native Americans. All others are immigrants or descendants of immigrants. Various ethnic, cultural, and social groups came to America to seek new opportunities and start a new life. English, Scottish, Irish and Germans farmers, Polish and Russian Jews, Italians, Norwegians, Swedes, Arabs, Chinese, Mexicans, Cubans and many more left their homelands for a number of different reasons – to escape from dictatorships, from religious persecution, unjust class systems, from famine and poverty. On a general level, we can distinguish three periods of immigration to North America: early immigration, European immigration in the 19th century, and immigration today.

Early Immigration

It is usually accepted that early immigration to North America started with the arrival of the first European settlers in the 17th century. It is true that America was not an empty waste of land when they came. 20,000 years earlier the very first settlers had arrived on the North American continent from eastern Asia, via Alaska and in 1492 Columbus and his ships had reached the **New World**, but it was the arrival of the **Pilgrim Fathers** on their ship **Mayflower** in 1620, which started the building of the American nation as we know it today.

The Pilgrims, who fled from religious persecution, began with the colonisation of the New England states. The first settlements were financed by so-called chartered companies, which had been provided by their governments with special rights and privileges. In the course of time, British, French and Spaniards took possession of great parts of North America, with their diverging political and economic interests eventually resulting in the colonists' **War of Independence** and the birth of the United States of America. During the one hundred years after the American Revolution (1776–1783) tides of newcomers flooded the country, and immigration on a large scale set in.

Large-scale Immigration in the 19th Century

The 19th century was the century of European immigration. Hundreds of thousands of small farmers, craftsmen and unskilled workers decided to leave their homelands and look for a better life in the United States, the land of freedom and opportunity. There were **three great waves of immigration** in the 19th century. The first wave between 1820 and 1860 brought immigrants from Great Britain, Ireland, and western Germany. During the second wave (1860 to 1890) the British, Irish and German groups were joined by immigrants from Scandinavian countries: During the third wave, from 1890 till 1915, the majority of newcomers were from southern and eastern Europe, from Greece, Italy, Austria, Hungary, Poland and Russia. With the outbreak of the First World War and the introduction of quotas in 1921 the uncontrolled inflow came to an end. The great time of immigration was over.

Reasons for Immigration

Although the incentives for emigration were varied, one of the main reasons why people left their homes in the Old World was the **search of a life in peace and freedom.** In the 17th century the Pilgrims fled from religious persecution and in the 20th century millions sought shelter from tyranny and political suppression in Nazi Germany and the Communist bloc countries. John F. Kennedy, 35th President of the USA, who was assassinated in 1963, was proud of America's history as a nation of immigrants: "America has always been a refuge from tyranny". Kennedy, himself a descendant of Irish immigrants, advocated a generous immigration policy. He was convinced that, especially in Communist countries, people were still oppressed and that the United States should keep the doors open for refugees from all over the world. American presidents, no matter what political party they belonged to, have frequently played the role of universal defender of people's liberty. In the 1980s, President Reagan criticized the Soviet Union for its disrespect of human rights and during his visit to Berlin he urged Soviet leader Mikhail Gorbachew: "Mr Gorbachew, tear down this wall." In the 1990s Presidents Bush and Clinton expressed their concern about the anti-democratic development in China following the Chinese government's cruel suppression of a student protest in Beijing's Tiananmen Square.

Another driving force behind immigration was the people's hope for **economic improvement**. In the middle of the 19th century the increased use of machinery in agriculture and the mechanization of the production process in the factories had made thousands of farm workers and craftsmen unemployed. On the other side of the Atlantic, however, the demand for cheap labour had increased at the same time. The **Civil War (1861–1865)** and the growth of the railroad system spurred industrialisation in the United States. The army needed large amounts of manufactured goods, such as rifles, uniforms and all sorts of supplies. The building of the railroads opened up the vast country, making the transportation of heavy loads over large distances possible. As a consequence, the American industry grew and expanded rapidly, with factories springing up everywhere. Manufacturers needed more and more workers and many of them advertised in European newspapers, even offering to pay the fare for would-be emigrants. The call was heard all over Europe. Thousands packed up their families and belongings in Ireland in the 1840s to escape from the **potato famine** which hit the country. In Germany people disillusioned with the slow process of improvement in the living standard for the lower classes left. Because of the continuous industrialisation, large numbers of immigrants were allowed into the United States to supply the much wanted labour. It was a give and take.

The work teams of Union Pacific Railroad and the Pacific Railroad lines met in Promontory, Utah to complete the first American transcontinental railway line.

Hunters and trappers were the first whites to move into the wild open spaces of the unknown territories in the Far West.

Once the newcomers had made some progress in their new home country they wrote to family and friends back home to report on their successes. The so-called **America letters** were published in Europe and became popular bestsellers. Recent immigrants gave glowing accounts of life in the New World, describing their new home country as a classless society with high wages, low prices, good land and a democratic government. "I would not press anyone to come but I will say they cannot provide so comfortable for their families in England as they can here with any given capital ... but my earnest wish is, to see all that I love and respect in this land of liberty where ... they might enjoy the fruit of their labour ..." (John Ingle, from Princeton, Indiana to England,

In Europe, steamship lines published posters to promote their profitable business of shipping immigrants across the Atlantic into the New World.

Aug 28, 1818). Reports like these, together with the propaganda of the steamship lines which promoted their profitable business of transporting the immigrants across the seas, attracted more newcomers.

Others came because they were **looking for adventure** in a country where there seemed to be no limits imposed by some governing authority, a country where there was room enough for people to lead a life according to their very personal preferences. Still others were attracted by the **lure of nature** – the wilderness possessed a certain magic which led many people to think of America as the new "Garden of Eden". Endless prairies and huge fertile valleys promised excellent conditions for farmers who fled from tiny strips of land in their home country. Thomas Jefferson believed that contact with nature led to a virtuous life. Therefore, he idealized the **yeoman farmer** and his sacred plough.

The "Huddled Masses"

The millions of poor and suppressed people who sought and found asylum in the New World are often referred to as the "huddled masses". This term is taken from a famous poem by Emma Lazarus, "The New Colossus", which is inscribed on a tablet inside the pedestal of the **Statue of Liberty**, the majestic copper figure in a long, flowing robe, standing at the entry to New York Harbour.

In commemoration of the hundredth anniversary of American independence in 1876 Emma Lazarus wrote her poem and the French government presented an enormous statue as a gift to the United States symbolizing the love of democracy in both countries. The sculpture, standing 46 m high on a 45.7 m pedestal, and weighing 204,000 kg, was created in the studio of the French sculptor Frederic Auguste Bartholdi. The figure wears a crown with spikes, representing the continents, and in her left carries a tablet bearing the inscription "July 4, 1776", the date on which the **Declaration of Independence** was proclaimed. On October 28, 1886, the statue was erected and since then refugees have been welcomed to their new home country by the sight of the imposing statue holding a torch into the air – which explains its full name: "Liberty Enlightening the World".

Journey across the Sea

In the 1890s the fare from Bremen to New York was 33 dollars – an enormous sum for the mostly poor emigrants. But their hopes and their dreams spurred them on and gave them the necessary strength to put up with the sometimes dangerous and always uncomfortable journey across the Atlantic. On the great steamships of the Cunard and White Star shipping lines 2,000 steerage passengers were jammed together below deck for the two-week crossing, enduring almost unbearable conditions. They slept on hard bunk beds, it was dark and freezing cold, the smell was awful, rats scampered around. One in ten did not survive the crossing and died of cholera, yellow fever, dysentery or smallpox.

Arrival in the New World

New York was the main entry point for mass immigration by sea. The great steamships arrived here with their loads of hopeful immigrants. Many newcomers stayed in New York, making it into the "City of the World (for all races are here, all the lands of the earth make contributions here)" – in the words of the American poet Walt Whitman –, a symbol of immigrant enterprise and ethnic integration. Racial tensions between the newcomers from different races, cultures and traditions did not exist, as all immigrants were united in the common aim to improve their living conditions. However, most of the poor newcomers had a difficult start in New York. The cheapest accommodation was available in the city's Lower East Side, where families crammed into tiny rooms without ventilation, daylight or running water. Men and women worked at least for 14 hours every day in **sweatshop factories** of the textile industry, only earning between three and ten dollars a week. "In this republican country, amid the fluctuating waves of our social life," once wrote Nathaniel Hawthorne, "somebody is always at drowning point."

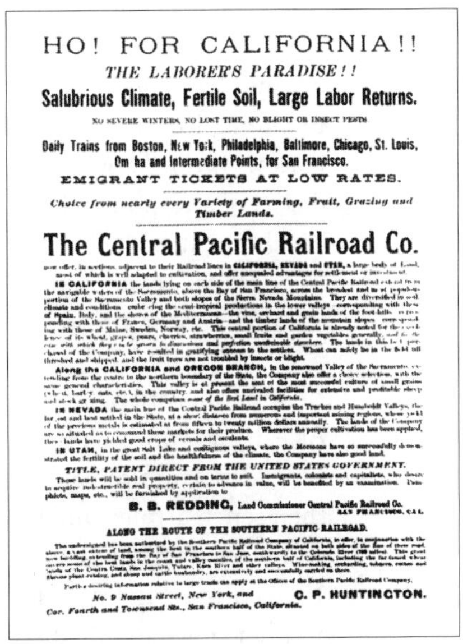

Railroad companies, eager for settlers to populate the West, advertised farmland for immigrants.

The first official immigration center at Ellis Island was opened in 1892.

More than 17 million immigrants arrived at the "The Isle of Hope".

When towards the end of the 19th century the tide of immigration from southern and eastern Europe began to flood the country, the older immigrants from northern Europe were calling for restrictions to bar the newcomers whom they scorned as "brutish, ill-smelling alien hordes". In response to this call for restrictions, the US immigration authorities opened the first official Federal immigration centre at **Ellis Island** in 1892. For more than 17 million men, women and children who were allowed into the country the processing centre became **"The Isle of Hope"**. Each week thousands had to go through the terrifying immigration routine – medical inspection and psychological examination. Immigrants who showed any signs of illness, especially contagious diseases, and politically doubtful characters or convicts were sent back home on the next boat. For these few – about 2 per cent – Ellis Island turned into "The Isle of Tears". Today the place where desperate people landed in the New World has been turned into a museum.

Germans in America

As early as 1683 the first German immigrants, who wanted to start a new life, arrived in America. They were **Pietists** and **Mennonites** who had suffered from the French armies under King Louis XIV or were persecuted by the Lutherans and other sects because of religious reasons. Queen Anne of England (1665–1714) offered them asylum and tens of thousands of Germans fled to England and her colonies. Most Germans settled in Pennsylvania (named by Charles II after his dead friend Admiral Penn, father of William Penn, 1644–1718) and made Germantown an important place for handicraft. Other Germans moved to New York or New Jersey (New Brunswick). The German Baron Friedrich Wilhelm von Steuben helped to form a disciplined army for General Washington to win the Revolutionary War.

In the 19th century about 6 million Germans emigrated to the United States because of crop failure and famine, political and social upheaval and religious persecution. Those who had sold their possessions in Germany came with enough money to buy farms from Americans who were about to move further west. Later on, many Germans moved to cities, particularly New York, St. Louis, Chicago and Cincinnati. The unskilled workers took any job available, but a high number of German immigrants were able to practice their craft they had learned back home: tailoring, baking, bookbinding, making furniture. Very soon and very quickly German immigrants were able to raise their standard of living, making German Americans the most successful of all non-English speaking immigrants by World War I. Of particular importance were German contributions in the fields of science, engineering, music and education.

A very special group of immigrants from German-speaking countries (Alsace, Switzerland and southern Germany) who today have become a tourist attraction for visitors to Pennsylvania are the **Amish**, a conservative Christian group founded by Jakob Ammann in the 17th century. The Amish began migrating to North America early in the 18th century and have preserved their characteristic non-conformist lifestyle, which reflects their obedience to biblical teachings. Members of the Amish community wear the same sort of plain clothes worn by their ancestors in the 17th century – broad-brimmed black hats for men, all of whom wear beards, and bonnets and long full dresses with capes for women. The Amish run and work their farms in a very traditional way without modern agricultural methods or machinery. They reject the blessings of modern technology. There are no telephones or electric lights, they drive horses and buggies rather than cars or lorries. Amish parents send their children to public elementary schools, but do not allow them to go on to high schools – a practice which has caused confrontations with the American authorities because of the compulsory school attendance laws. Some Amish parents have gone to jail rather than allow their children to go to high school.

The American Dream

"From rags to riches, from dishwasher to millionaire" – the hope of self-improvement and success is traditionally expressed in the term "American Dream". For many it has been a vision, an aspiration – and for others an illusion. Some of the immigrants who emigrated to the United States believed that in the "the land of promise" the streets would be paved with gold. The more realistic immigrants, however, simply hoped for a better life. They firmly believed that in America personal success was possible and within reach of each individual because of the social, economic and political conditions for hard-working people. The American Dream implies **liberty**, **justice** and the **pursuit of happiness**, as expressed in the **American Declaration of Independence of 1776**.

The belief and trust in personal achievement based on private initiative has become the foundation of American politics. However, this dream of a democratic and prosperous society guaranteeing "liberty and justice for all" has not yet been achieved for all groups in America. In the 1960s, in his famous speech "I have a dream" Martin Luther King referred to the ideal of equality as "a dream deeply rooted in the American Dream" and expressed his optimism that it would come true for black people too. In 1997, in his Inaugural Speech for his second term of office President Clinton reprimanded the American people to continue striving for the realisation of the American Dream for all Americans: "Martin Luther King's dream was the American Dream."

In our modern world it has become much harder to follow the American Dream and to achieve success. If personal accomplishment is the guiding social principle what will become of those people who, for whatever reason, are unable to achieve it? People who are unable to attain success in a competitive world are regarded as losers. Willy Loman, the main character in Arthur Miller's play *Death of a Salesman*, experiences the darker side of the American Dream. Loman firmly believes in the American Dream and clings on to the values of old pioneering days. He refuses to accept that the extraordinary opportunities which were once open to the pioneers no longer exist. The failure of sensitive people to live with their unfulfilled dreams and frustrations is also a central theme in the plays of Tennessee Williams (1911–1981). Williams portrays women in crises who act under the influence of an illusionary view both of themselves and their world. In *The Glass Menagerie* (1944) Amanda, a domineering mother, yearns for the return of a romantic past, when she was a popular young lady and Laura withdraws into a fantasy world with a collection of glass animals. Blanche DuBois, the main character in *A Streetcar Named Desire* (1947), is unable to accept that the old world in which her family was well-off and ran a plantation has crumbled. Just as she is about to take faltering steps to re-build her life, the brutal Stanley Kowalski, in his ignorance and insensitivity, destroys her hopes and her illusions. The only way out for Blanche is to retreat into insanity. For people like Willy Loman, Amanda and Laura Wingfield and Blanche DuBois, who live with false pretences because they cannot cope with the harsh realities of life, the American Dream has turned into a nightmare.

The Frontier

In the view of the settlers, the "**frontier**" was the dividing line between the white settlements and, as they saw it, the free unoccupied land, beyond. It was the border country between civilisation and "the wilderness". The early colonists had built their homes and cities on the east coast, but very soon adventurers like Daniel Boone began to explore and open up new lands outside the boundaries, first north and then west, eventually to the Pacific coast. In 1803, President Thomas Jefferson ordered an expedition led by Lewis and Clark to trace the Mississippi River to its source and to find the best way to the Pacific Ocean. The report of the successful expedition, published in 1814, informed the American public about the potential of the territories in the **Far West**.

Fifty years later, after the end of the **Civil War** in 1865, the move west began, pushing the frontier further and further into unknown territory. The driving forces behind the **westward-movement** were the quest for cheap land and natural resources, economic opportunities, better living conditions for families and self-improvement. The first whites to move into the unknown were the hunters and **trappers**, followed by the backwoods settlers who were half hunters, half farmers. Then came the **farmers**, many of them optimistic and idealistic immigrants from Europe, who were drawn into the wilderness by the abundance of land. The main lines of migration came from the East and South. Important routes like the Santa Fe Trail and the Oregon Trail, both of which followed old Indian paths, opened new lands to adventurous and daring pioneers. A favourite starting point was the town of Independence in Missouri. Many pioneers set out from there in their rough wagons on a 3,000 km overland route which took them down the Missouri River, through the **Great Plains** across the Rocky Mountains and finally into Oregon. People took time in migrating to the West, pausing for a year or more in several places before reaching their final destination. When settlements eventually grew in size and villages and towns developed, the third wave of the pioneer movement arrived. Merchants, doctors, bankers and lawyers came to provide services to the growing population.

The building of a system of **railroad** lines across the continent and the discovery of **gold in California** played an important part in the settlement of the Far West. When in 1848 James Marshall found nuggets of gold in a river in northern California, the news spread like wildfire, and more than 100,000 miners poured into the country. Some prospectors struck it rich, others were less lucky, but eventually stayed in the new land. In 1859 reports of gold and silver discoveries in Colorado and Nevada caused an influx of fortune hunters.

Realizing the overall importance of a reliable and efficient transport system, the American government encouraged railway companies to lay tracks across the United States by giving them free land and financial support. The Union Pacific Railroad started in the east, the Pacific Railroad in the west, in California. When both lines met in Promontory in Utah, the first transcontinental railway line was completed. In the short time of 30 years, between 1870 and 1900, the whites had settled more land than in the 150 years before. They had taken over 430 million acres of the land west of the Mississippi, thus completing the conquest of the West, America's frontier.

The Pioneering Spirit

Frederick Jackson Turner was among the first American historians to explain how deeply the conquest of the frontier influenced the development of the American nation and the character of its people. Ever since the initial colonization of the continent, the American people have been a "people in motion" and mobility has become a unique trait that distinguishes Americans from Europeans. Charles Dickens saw the West as "peopled by a vast human army, consisting of people who had dedicated their lives to leaving home after home behind."

Since the days of the frontier movement Americans have always placed high value on independence, self-confidence and individualism – the virtues of pioneer life. When seen from the positive side, the pioneering spirit has promoted people's ability to adapt to new circumstances and to overcome difficulties through private initiative and invention. On the other hand, however, in many heroic frontier stories and Hollywood Western movies the pioneers' individualism was reduced to a frequent use of guns and trigger-happy gunmen set the scene. These colourful pageants paint a distorted picture of the past because in reality the pioneers made little use of rifles and revolvers – most of them were farmers and homesteaders who were completely inexperienced in the handling of weapons. However, the glorification of the gun led to a culture of weaponry, where firearms were regarded as symbols of freedom and power. Not surprisingly therefore, America's gun laws are more permissive than in any other nation and weapons can be bought fairly easily. The consequences of this liberal way with firearms are evident: In 1997, 12,397 people were killed by firearms in the United States, compared to 64 in Britain. Whenever there are lethal shootings in American schools for example, sensible people question the individual's right to purchase and carry a gun and politicians call for stricter gun control. Up to now , however, all efforts have been squashed by the powerful National Rifle Association, which aims at "protecting firearms freedoms and promoting shooting sports" and the right of "law-abiding citizens to own and use firearms for legitimate purposes." In 1960 John F. Kennedy used the word "frontier" in the meaning of 'a challenge which the whole American nation must face'.

The Fate of the Native Americans

The conquest of the West, America's colonial empire, was a triumph for the independent, optimistic, hard-working settlers, and a tragedy for the continent's original inhabitants, the American Indians. The frontier movement ended in a genocide of the native people of America, diminishing their population to a mere 200,000 through fighting, disease and starvation.

In the beginning, the relationship between the first white Europeans and the Indians was friendly and the settlers depended on the help of the natives to survive in a hostile environment. However, the situation changed as more and more "sod-busters" – the farmers who cleared the land and started their farms in the wilderness – tracked west and occupied Indian territory. They drove the natives relentlessly off the land of their ancestors, killing thousands who were unwilling to make room and be moved into reservations, usually barren, infertile grounds the whites did not want. To justify the cleansing of the Indians the concept of "**Manifest Destiny**" was propagated, according to which it was the Godly mission of the white man to conquer the virgin wilderness and civilize the racially inferior and culturally primitive "savages".

The myth of "Manifest Destiny" helped push waves of American settlers westward to the Pacific, displacing native peoples and devastating their culture and traditional way of life. The resistance the Indians put up against the white invaders was weak, as the Indians were not united among themselves and tribal warfare was frequent. The greatest Indian victory was won in 1876 when Sioux warriors defeated and annihilated the 7th Cavalry commanded by the over-ambitious and reckless George Armstrong Custer at Little Bighorn. Most of the time, however, Indian uprisings, which were often protests against the fact that the whites had broken earlier concluded treaties or promises, were crushed with utter brutality during the Indian wars in the second half of the 19th century. Subsequent federal government **Indian policies** always safeguarded the interests of the whites and neglected those of the original inhabitants. Laws like the **General Allotment Act** of 1887, also called Dawes Act, facilitated the acquisition of land for the white settlers and the Indians were moved into ever smaller reservations.

In the 20th century Indian policy of the government aimed at the integration of native Americans into urban centres, thus hastening the termination, and extinction, of tribes. These efforts at forced assimilation ("termination policy") were not successful, however, and given up in the 1960s by the Johnson administration. Since the 1970s, after Indian protestors had occupied Alcatraz Island in San Francisco Bay to alarm the public about the misery of the disadvantaged Indians, a new policy, called "self-determination", has been in effect. It has kept the protective role of the federal government – providing Indians with education and various forms of support – and has increased the participation of the tribes in important areas of local government.

Trying to secure a place in today's modern world: native Americans.

Many Indians live from tourism or farming, urban Indians accept all sorts of menial jobs.

About one-third of today's 2 million native Americans (about 0.8 per cent of the total US population) live on one of the 280 reservations. Where natural resources (coal, oil, natural gas or uranium) are found, the Indians lease out exploitation rights to white companies, others live from farming or tourism. Some tribes run casinos, the profits of which go back to the members. The urban Indians try to survive in the cities accepting all sorts of menial jobs. The living conditions of the majority of American Indians are still appalling, despite efforts of the **Department of Housing and Urban Development** (HUD). Unemployment, alcoholism and frequent disease are constant threats, which altogether make the Indians the **poorest ethnic group** in the USA. In spite of all this there is a silver lining on the horizon. On many reservations Indians make efforts to revive their tribal heritage, their languages and religious ceremonies and restore in their children the pride of belonging to the continent's original inhabitants.

20th Century Immigration

Hispanic Immigration

By 1910 the great period of immigration was over, and after the political upheavals in Europe which resulted in two world wars the influx of legal migrants was finally brought to a halt. Congress passed new stricter immigration laws with set quotas for each country which de facto closed the doors to the United States. It took many years before immigrants were admitted again in greater numbers. Fifteen years after the end of World War II, in the 1960s, the US government changed its immigration policy. The government dropped racially based quotas on immigration and favoured immigration from Third World nations. Since then the number of coloured immigrants has risen considerably. For more than a century most of the new arrivals had come from Europe, from the 1960s onward would-be entrants came mainly from Asia and from the countries south of the border of the US.

In 1950 fewer than four million US residents were Hispanics – immigrants from Spanish-speaking countries such as Cuba, Mexico, or Puerto Rico. Today that number is about 27 million, which makes the Hispanic population in the United States the fifth-largest in the world – after Mexico, Spain, Colombia and Argentina. 36 per cent of the Hispanics in the United States live in California and you can hear Spanish spoken in all parts of Los Angeles. Hundreds of thousands of Cubans fleeing the Castro regime have settled in Miami. So many Cuban Americans live there that the *Miami Herald,* the city's largest newspaper, publishes separate editions in English and Spanish. On the whole, Hispanic immigrants tend to have lower levels of education and consequently lower incomes than the majority of the American population and other immigrant groups, the most successful of which are the Asians.

Asian Immigration

The Chinese were the first ethnic group to be affected by immigration laws towards the end of the 19th century. They had come to the US in such large numbers that people in America feared the Chinese would take away jobs. Prejudice against Asians and fear of the so-called "yellow peril" were so strong that anti-Chinese riots broke out in 1880. Two years later Congress passed the first of the **Chinese Exclusion Acts** which barred Chinese "coolies" ('Hilfsarbeiter') from immigration to the United States and excluded Chinese from naturalization. It took 50 years before the laws that kept out Chinese immigrants were repealed (1943), and legislation passed in 1952 allowed not only Asians but people of all races to become US citizens. As a consequence the inflow from the Far East increased. Many came as refugees in the 1970s after the end of the Vietnam war. Today about 10 million people are of Asian descent and Asian Americans are one of the fastest-growing ethnic groups. More than 40 per cent of them live in the big cities of Los Angeles, New York and San Francisco. More recently, Las Vegas and Atlanta have become favourite destinations, too. As to the socio-economic standing of Asian immigrants, the same pattern as in Britain can be observed. Asians are among the most successful of all immigrant groups. They have a higher income than many other ethnic groups, and large numbers of their children study at the best US universities as undergraduate and postgraduate students.

Because of the influx of non-European immigrants **America's racial structure** has already changed. In the 21st century the population of the United States will continue to grow increasingly diverse, with Asia and Central America remaining the major sources of immigration. In the year 2006, the Hispanic population will outnumber the black population. By 2050, approximately 53 per cent of the population in the United States will be White, 25 per cent Hispanic, 14 per cent Black, 8 per cent Asian, and 1 per cent American Indian.

Attitudes towards Immigration

In the early days of mass immigration, most newcomers were welcomed because they contributed to the success of the new-born nation that desperately needed more strong hands to conquer its vast territory and build its economy. Today, Americans are divided in their attitude towards immigration. According to a recent poll, two-thirds of the population would like to reduce it, but, strangely enough, the same proportion think that legal immigration is a good thing. People who see immigration in a less positive light complain about the cost of the newcomers to the state, their contributions to crime and disease, about the burdens on schools and welfare rolls. The swift success of many immigrants has caused a good deal of envy, resentment, growing discrimination and even outright hostility and violence against newcomers – in particular against illegal undocumented aliens.

Illegal Immigration

Somewhat less than a million immigrants arrive in the United States each year. Of these, 700,000 enter as lawful permanent residents and another 100,000 to 150,000 enter legally as refugees or others fleeing persecution. Undocumented immigrants constitute only 1 per cent of the total US population and, contrary to popular belief, most of these immigrants do not enter the United States illegally by crossing the border with Canada or Mexico. Six out of ten illegal immigrants enter the US legally with a student, tourist, or business visa and become illegal when they stay in the United States after their visas expire. Since the 1960s the number of undocumented Mexicans who come to the US by crossing the Rio Grande – hence their nickname "**wetbacks**" – has been on the increase. It is reckoned that for every would-be entrant arrested at the southern border between two to ten others successfully slip through. When they first came, these people found jobs as temporary or migrant workers, working on a seasonal basis harvesting crops in the fields of California. Today, however, more and more illegal aliens are no longer satisfied with menial jobs. They have acquired qualifications and apply for better-paid jobs such as carpenters, bricklayers and machine operators. This is why local citizens see the competition of the immigrants as a threat to their own chances on the job market. It is this increasing number of illegal immigrants which worries ordinary people and which has caused social tension between Americans and aliens. Right-wing politicians try to introduce new laws and tighten the regulations under which aliens are admitted in order to cut down the number of newcomers.

Melting Pot or Salad Bowl?

Traditionally, the United States has been regarded as a melting pot where immigrants from many different cultures, races, and religions have been assimilated and moulded into "the first universal nation". People no longer felt German, Italian, Polish or Irish – they thought of themselves as Americans, as members of a truly multicultural society. During the 19th century, when most immigrants came from Europe, assimilation was not difficult because the newcomers looked like the Americans and were able to blend in unobtrusively. However, two factors have brought about a change so that now more and more cracks in the melting pot are being discovered. First of all since the shift in US immigration policy in the late 1960s, when the government dropped racially based quotas on immigration, the number of coloured immigrants has risen considerably. Sociologists have described this process as the "**browning of America**". Secondly, not all non-European immigrants wish to assimilate into the American culture, they do not want to discard their customs and traditions. They take pride in their ethnic heritage and wish to pass it on to their children as well, and – above all – they want to keep their mother tongue. In many parts of the south-western and south-eastern United States English already plays a secondary role because most newcomers are keeping to their Spanish. In Florida and California non-melting tendencies are most obvious. Latinos have their own theatres, cinemas, television channels, restaurants, bars, and in most schools **bilingualism** – teaching in two languages – is firmly established.

Every year about 1.2 million immigrants want to become Americans and apply for naturalisation. Having passed a test on the basics of American citizenship, history and culture, they swear allegiance to the flag. However, the old view of the nation as a melting pot is no longer true and many people are beginning to refer to it as a myth. **Multiculturalists** – people who are convinced of the advantages of a multi-cultural society – have given up using the term "melting pot" because of the word's underlying meaning of 'enforced assimilation'. Today most people prefer to see the United States as a **salad bowl**, or a **fruit salad** – a combination of many cultures, living and working together, each distinct and separate in itself. The ingredients can still clearly be identified, which means the immigrant groups have kept their ethnicity. The majority of the immigrants tried very hard to reach the land of their dreams, some even had to sacrifice their lives. Once admitted the question is not so much as whether to integrate completely into the American society and adopt the American way of life as whether to keep one's ethnic identity. Most important is that the immigrants assimilate enough. e. g. by learning the language to take full advantage of the possibilities which their new homeland offers. Today most people would still agree that the melting pot USA should allow all the flavours to mix. Immigrants from all parts of the world have given America its cultural diversity that has made it a great nation – even if accommodating the newcomers often brings problems.

The Civil Rights Movement in the USA

What is the Civil Rights Movement?

When we talk about the **Civil Rights Movement** in the United States, we refer to the protests against racial segregation and discrimination of blacks in the Deep South. In the 1950s and 1960s the fight for equal and fair treatment became an important issue. Through the leadership of the Baptist minister **Martin Luther King** the campaign for equality gained momentum and was turned into a mass movement. King's methods of **non-violent direct action** (the organisation of boycotts, sit-ins, demonstrations and protest marches) were increasingly supported not only by black but also by white Americans. The Civil Rights Movement achieved two great victories with the passage of the **Civil Rights Act** of 1964 and the V**oting Rights Act** of 1965, which recognized black Americans as equal citizens and secured their right to vote.

Civil rights are the freedoms and privileges given to a citizen of a country; among these are the rights to political and social freedom and job equality irrespective of a person's sex, race or religion. **Human rights,** on the other hand, are the rights belonging fundamentally to all people, i.e. the basic freedoms that all human beings should have from childhood on (e.g. the right of life, the right to say what you think or to travel freely). Although the Civil Rights Movement will always be connected with the name of Martin Luther King, the struggle for the emancipation of black Americans has a long tradition.

The Beginnings of Slavery and Segregation

For hundreds of years blacks in America were called "Negroes" (even worse, abused as "Niggers"), then, in the 1960s, they were referred to as "blacks" or "black Americans", but today they themselves prefer the politically correct term "**African Americans**" to remind everyone of their origin and the fact that they did not come to America of their own free will, but, in the words of John F. Kennedy, "were bought and sold and had no choice".

Voyage into Slavery

In the early 17th century the slave trade between the African and the American continent began. British vessels transported natives from African countries like Sierra Leone to the Caribbean and the Southern states of America where they were sold as slaves to work on the cotton, tobacco and sugar plantations. Not all of the captured black people survived the journey on the tightly packed ships. The weak ones who could not endure the appalling conditions on the ships were thrown overboard. "Sharks had learnt that following the slave ships was the way to grow fat", Malcolm X said later. By the time the United States was founded in 1783, slavery was practised in all of the 13 original colonies. Although the **Declaration of Independence** clearly stated that "all men are created equal", the principle of equality did not include blacks, as the Negroes slaves were not regarded as "men" or "people" nor were they citizens of the United States. Moreover, the slaves were a welcome source of cheap labour and had contributed greatly to the wealth of the South. So slavery was an important economic factor and influential plantation and slave owners were not willing to renounce that privilege.

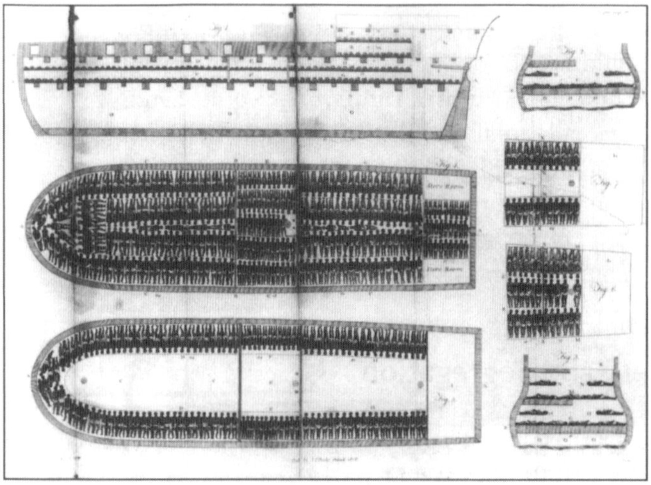

Slave traders transported blacks from the West Coast of Africa to the Southern states of America where they were sold to work on the plantations. The slaves were packed tightly below deck and kept in chains day and night. Those who died during the sea passage were thrown overboard.

North versus South: Free at last?

In the early 19th century slavery and the treatment of blacks as second-class citizens came under heavy criticism. Anti-slavery associations were formed, which raised moral questions about slavery and advocated the abolition of that inhuman form of exploitation. The argument between the North and the South about this question contributed to the outbreak of the **American Civil**

War (1861–1865), although, in reality, the war was essentially about economic and political power. The rural South believed in its right to leave the Union ("secession") and wanted to keep slavery as its agriculture depended to a large extent on the black labour force. The growing industries in the North, on the other hand, were able to recruit enough workers from the ranks of the masses of European immigrants who were arriving from across the Atlantic. As a result of the victory of the Northern states in the conflict slavery was finally abolished. President Lincoln's 1863 **Emancipation Proclamation** declared slaves free. The **Thirteenth Amendment** (1865) to the US Constitution abolished slavery forever and the Fourteenth Amendment of 1868 extended US citizenship to all former slaves.

Slavery is replaced by Segregation

Despite these legal achievements, the situation of the black Americans in the South did not change for the better and racial discrimination continued. Slavery was followed by segregation of whites and blacks, with "separate but equal" facilities. That means that businesses and public accommodations were segregated according to race. In buses, trains, restaurants, hotels, schools, theatres and even jails there were special sections reserved for whites and others for blacks, so that both groups would not meet and mix. The highest court of the country, the US Supreme Court, legitimised in a landmark decision of 1896 the practice of "separate but equal" facilities for the races. As a matter of fact, more and more rules were introduced to enforce segregation. The so-called "**Jim Crow Laws**" were passed, officially for the protection of the blacks, but in reality the regulations were used to maintain the unfair treatment and the limitation of the rights of the black part of the population. Originally, "Jim Crow" was the name of a song-and-dance act, but the expression came to be used as an insulting name for blacks in general. Because of the "Jim Crow" practices, black people in the South were denied equal opportunities in employment and, above all, the right to vote. Consequently they remained the powerless victims of discrimination.

Winds of Change after World War II

During the first half of the 20th century little progress was made in fighting for racial equality, however, the winds of change began to blow after the end of World War II. In the North blacks had acquired a certain wealth and from their economic achievements they drew enough confidence to press for their full rights as citizens of the US. Internationally, the United States had committed itself to the defence of freedom and democracy for all mankind, heavily criticising the racist ideology of Nazi Germany and the disregard of human rights in the Communist bloc. Thoughtful whites criticised the American hypocrisy, pointing to the contradiction between what the US required from others and what it practised at home. In 1948, President Truman ordered the desegregation of the armed forces, in view of the fact that blacks had fought bravely as US soldiers in the war.

In 1954 the United States **Supreme Court** took a historic decision. In the legal case Oliver Brown versus Board of Education of Topeka, Kansas, the Supreme Court decided unanimously on May 17, 1954 that the "separate but equal" concept was unconstitutional, thus overthrowing its ruling of 1896. This decision not only paved the way for school desegregation but also marks the beginning of a mass movement of black and white sympathisers to end the segregationist practises and racial inequalities across the nation and particularly in the South.

Martin Luther King and the Civil Rights Movement

Montgomery Bus Boycott

It was a small incident in Montgomery, Alabama, which triggered off a mass protest and gave the Civil Rights Movement new impetus. On a cold December evening in 1955, forty-two-year-old Rosa Parks, who worked as a seamstress in a factory, was on her way home from work riding on a bus. According to the strict segregation rules of the Montgomery City Bus Lines black passengers had to sit in the back and had to give up their seats if the white section in the front of the bus became occupied. Ms Parks was sitting in the first row of the rear section designated for blacks. It was a busy day and when the white section of the bus was filled, the driver ordered Ms Parks to give up her seat for a white man. The tired woman was fed up with being treated like a second-class citizen, she refused and was arrested. The news of her arrest aroused the leaders of the black community to action. They met at Dexter Avenue Baptist Church to discuss the issue. Among them was a young minister, 28-year-old Martin Luther King Jr., who had been pastor in Montgomery for little more than a year. It was agreed to start a bus boycott in protest against segregated seating on the city buses. The boycott eventually lasted much longer than anyone had expected – 381 days – and the bus company lost 65 per cent of its income. Eight months later, the Supreme Court decided that bus segregation violated the constitution. Because of the non-violent way he had conducted the boycott, Martin Luther King had in little more than a year become one of the nation's most remarkable leaders of the Civil Rights Movement.

The March on Washington

On August 28, 1963, King led a march on Washington to commemorate the signing of the Emancipation Proclamation by Abraham Lincoln at the end of the Civil War in 1863. Exactly one hundred years had passed since slavery was abolished, but blacks still did not enjoy the same rights as whites. The march culminated in a mass demonstration in the mall between the Lincoln Memorial and the Washington Monument. In front of a crowd of more than 250,000 Americans, including 60,000 whites, King delivered one of the greatest speeches in American history, his famous "I Have a Dream" speech.

Many disillusioned black Americans regarded Martin Luther King's (right) preaching of non-violent resistance as too weak. They supported other civil rights activists such as Malcolm X (left) of the Black Power Movement who favored militant, aggressive protests.

"I Have a Dream"

In his address Martin Luther King referred to the words of the **Declaration of Independence** of 1776: "We hold these truths to be self-evident, that all men are created equal". By reminding his listeners of the principles laid down by the Founding Fathers he demanded the delivery of those promises: citizenship rights for the black Americans, justice, equality and freedom. King was optimistic that whites and blacks would one day be able to live together in peace, mutual respect and understanding. In his speech he conveyed his firm conviction that racial integration was the overall goal of the civil rights movement and he expressed his hopes of a **colour-blind America** where people would not be judged "by the colour of their skin but by the content of their character". Martin Luther King encouraged his listeners to keep up their spirits in spite of the frustrations of everyday life, despite the discrepancies between the ideal of the "land of the free" and the humiliating inequalities blacks were still confronted with.

Martin Luther King was one of the most powerful and skilful orators of the Civil Rights Movement. With his usage of poetic language ("mountain of despair"), his biblical phraseology ("every valley shall be exalted"), his repetition of keywords and keyphrases ("I have a dream") and parallel sentence structures he deeply impressed his audience. As a trained and experienced preacher he used elements of a Negro sermon, encouraging the participation of his listeners whom he addressed as "friends". King had prepared his speech in writing but as he was speaking he himself became so emotional and cheered by the immediate response of his audience that he improvised great parts of his speech. Still today "I Have a Dream" has retained all its vigour and freshness.

"[...] I say to you today, my friends, so even though we face the difficulties of today and tomorrow, I still have a dream. It is a dream deeply rooted in the American dream."

Martin Luther King was assassinated at his motel in Memphis on April 4, 1968. These words from a spiritual song which he had quoted in his address "I Have a Dream" are carved on his tombstone: "At last, free at last, thank God Almighty, I'm free at last."

King's Method of Non-violent Resistance

Influenced by his studies of the successful methods applied by Mahatma Gandhi and his Christian convictions as a clergyman Martin Luther King firmly believed in **non-violent action**. With demonstrations, sit-in campaigns and marches he wanted to make white Americans aware of the failure to extend civil rights to the black part of the population. The lethargic response from the whites and the slow progress in the improvement of the living conditions caused younger blacks to become impatient and aggressive. Martin Luther King's tactics of non-violent resistance and civil disobedience were heavily attacked as being too lenient and too soft. One of the most outspoken critics was Malcolm X of the **Black Power Movement**.

The Militant Black Power Movement

Malcolm X, whose real name was Malcolm Little, was born in 1925 in Omaha, Nebraska, and had a very unhappy childhood. When he was six years old, his father was murdered by members of the Ku Klux Klan. His mother suffered a nervous breakdown and her eight children were taken into care by the welfare department. At 21, Malcolm got into trouble with the police, he was convicted of burglary and sentenced to prison. There he was introduced to the **Black Muslim Movement**. After his release in 1952, he changed his name to Malcolm X and became a leading personality of the Black Power Movement. In his **Black Panthers' Programme** he approved of violent actions against whites.

Malcolm X rejected Martin Luther King's peaceful tactics because he believed that racism should be opposed "by any means necessary" and consequently preached the violent way to solve America's race problem. He was convinced that the chasm between the races could never be bridged because all whites were evil and would never accept blacks on equal terms. The solution for the black man lay in racial separation, not integration. Therefore "the American black man should be focusing his every effort on building his own businesses, and decent homes for himself". Instead of putting all his hopes on integration by legal means like Martin Luther King had done, Malcolm X encouraged black people to work hard for economic success. Instead of relying on the white man's charity and generosity in the form of welfare payments blacks should lean on their own strength and try to stand on their own feet. This alone could bring back pride and self-esteem. After 1964 Malcolm X softened his aggressive and hateful attitude against whites and left the Black Muslims to form a rival group, the **Organization for Afro-American Unity**. In 1965 he was gunned down in New York by three assassins, two of whom were Black Muslims.

Where Does the Civil Rights Movement Stand Today?

Little Rock – Then and Now

In 1957 1,000 paratroopers and 10,000 National Guardsmen were needed to guarantee the admission of nine black students to an all-white High School. Today that same school has 1,800 students, 60 per cent of whom are black. This fact illustrates the achievements of the Civil Rights Movement after forty years of fighting for equality. On September 3, 1957, three years after the

Supreme Court's landmark decision of 1954 to end the practise of "separate but equal" facilities, a group of nine black teenage students arrived to enrol at Central High, an institution in Little Rock, Arkansas, which had always been reserved for whites, but the youngsters were refused admission. President Eisenhower ordered soldiers to Little Rock, and on September 25 the students were allowed to enrol and Central High School was desegregated. Even then, however, President Eisenhower himself, who by his action had enforced the rights of "**The Little Rock Nine**", said that legislation and government action alone could not bring about integration, because it could not change the people's hearts and overcome their suspicions and prejudices.

Affirmative Action

America did not become 'colour-blind', as Martin Luther King had hoped, people did not become more tolerant. More laws were needed to compensate for the injustices against blacks. Following the passing of the **Equal Opportunity and Employment Act** in 1972 the government encouraged a system of preferences to protect blacks (and women) from being discriminated against. The policy, which was called "**affirmative action**", required employers when they hired or contracted new staff to prefer applicants from ethnic minority groups even if candidates from those groups had lower test scores than white applicants. In recent years criticism of this system has increased. Whites complained of "reverse discrimination", and most people agreed that merit should be the only criterion for entry to a job and not race, sex or religion. Even members of minority groups, who were supposed to profit from affirmative action, were not pleased about the preferential system. Black conservatives said their people became addicted to racial preferences instead of hard work. Following that criticism, affirmative action has been abolished in some states.

Martin Luther King or Malcolm X?

Today many people in the US would agree that race relations are less than ideal, in fact, some observers say that the racial tension has increased and warn of a new race divide which could tear the United States apart. It is true, great sections of the black community have made economic and political progress in the past 40 years. There are also reports about more and more Americans marrying across the racial divide, a fact which seems to suggest that whites and blacks are burying their historic animosities. However, for the majority of African-Americans King's dream of harmonious and peaceful co-existence has not become reality. Consequently, outbursts of violence have become more frequent. Disillusioned blacks and members of other minority groups rioted in Los Angeles and other major cities in 1992, turning the American Dream into a nightmare. Martin Luther King's optimistic vision has been shattered by persistent discrimination, and racial integration seems further away than ever.

Many African American families still live in dire poverty and cannot buy the food, shelter, clothing, and medical care they need – despite the long fight for racial equality.

On The Road to Ethnic Separatism?

Thirty years after Martin Luther King's death new radical and militant black leaders raised their voices in protest and revived Malcolm X's doctrine of racial separatism. In 1995 Louis Farrakhan organized the biggest demonstration in the history of the United States: "The Million Man March" of black American men on Washington. Farrakhan preached Malcolm X's principle that blacks should stop being recipients of welfare and "do it for themselves". He wanted blacks off welfare and in business. In his view the two groups, blacks and whites, were worlds apart and their different attitudes were irreconcilable. Therefore they should "get a divorce", which means blacks and whites should live separately – perhaps one day even in separate states in the US.

This view is not shared by the more moderate black leaders in the **NAACP** (National Association for the Advancement of Colored People), still the US's largest black political organisation, which follows Martin Luther King's philosophy of reconciliation between the races. However, dissenters within this group are making themselves heard more often. They seriously question the idea of racial integration, pointing to the fact that blacks still are disproportionately poor and disadvantaged despite so many years of fighting for racial equality. President Clinton warned of a new race divide, saying "Any nation which indulges itself in **ethnic separatism** will not be able to master the challenges of the 21st century." And so the fight for equality and a united America has not yet come to an end.

Education

Education in the Information Age

Parents, teachers and politicians alike agree that providing a good education for the younger generation is of vital importance today. Politicians and economists stress the fact that the country needs a qualified work force which will be able to compete in the global economy. However, an adequate education is not only necessary to secure the nation's economic success it is also vital for each individual because the world of work is undergoing drastic changes. In the 1950s for instance, only 20 per cent of American jobs were classified as professional and 60 per cent as unskilled. In our modern world today, which increasingly relies on technology, the proportion of unskilled jobs has fallen to 20 per cent, while skilled jobs now account for at least 60 per cent of the workforce. Furthermore, the traditional view held in the past that school and work are distinct worlds is no longer valid. Learning has been turned into a lifelong activity and is no longer limited to the time spent at school. The kinds of jobs people had in former times did not require the kind of basic education and specialized training often required in the workforce today. Almost every job today increasingly requires a combination of academic knowledge and practical skills that need learning throughout a lifetime.

Whereas everybody agrees on the importance of education, opinions are divided as to how the quality of public education in the United States can be guaranteed and how standards can be raised. A basic question concerns the role of technology in the classroom. The rapid pace of technological change and the sheer volume of information available also present new challenges to educators, students and others involved in learning. The Internet gives people of all ages no matter where they attend school, or even if they do not attend a formal school, direct access to a vast number of informational sources around the world. Other issues discussed at present refer to the financing of schools, the establishment of national standards and testing in education, and the rising number of private schools. In addition, psychologists and sociologists doubt whether high academic performance alone should be the highest goal of schools and teaching staff. Alarmed by the rise of social evils, such as drugs and violence in the urban ghetto schools, educators demand a curriculum that touches more closely on contemporary social problems. They believe that character-building and social integration should take first place. Anyone who takes part in the debate about reforming the educational system recognises the fundamental role which the public school system played in forming the American nation. It was education, supplied by schools and colleges, which integrated generations of new immigrants into the New World and provided them with skills and knowledge to move upward within society. This function of education will become even more vital in the **multi-ethnic society** of today. The US classroom in primary and secondary schools is more diverse than at any time in the nation's history. To give an example, in 1972 6 per cent of students at American schools came from Hispanic families, by 1998 their number had increased to 15 per cent.

Decentralized School System

Some of the opportunities as well as many of the problems of education in the United States stem from the fact that the country's **public school system** is totally decentralized. There is no central federal agency or government department to control the whole system, nor is there a national curriculum. Although the **United States Cabinet** has a **Department of Education**, it has no authority over the operation of schools. The responsibility for education rests solely with the states in cooperation with local school districts. When the Founding Fathers drafted the Constitution they did not want to hand too much authority to a central federal government, and therefore reserved the right of individual states to control education. Consequently, when laws were passed making schooling compulsory – Massachusetts Bay Colony passed such a law in 1642 – responsibility for the schools was placed into the hands of local school boards, of which today there are about 30,000. They each independently select the principals/headmasters for their schools, the teachers and other personnel and decide on salaries. In order to provide funds for the newly founded schools the system of **property tax** was developed. This means that school boards raise money by taxing local homes or businesses at a certain rate. This system is still in operation today and leads to great inequalities, because the value of homes in different areas of a state varies greatly. When there are a lot of wealthy residents who can afford more expensive homes, the school board of this region will have more money available through property tax. This again means that these authorities can invest more in the schools they run, buying more computers and increasing teachers' salaries. On the whole, the funds raised by property tax are insufficient to cover school budgets, and this is where the federal government comes in. Although it has only an advisory function, today it provides more money for schools and school programmes than the local districts supply.

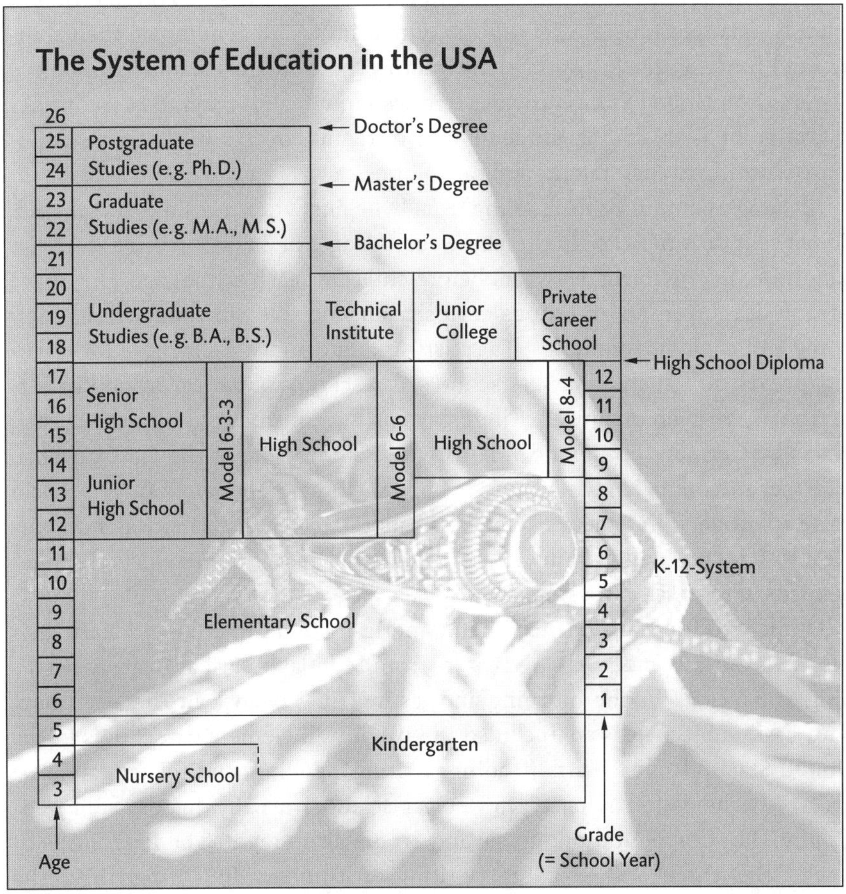

The K-12 System: From Kindergarten to High School

In the United States, as in most industrialised countries school attendance is compulsory. All American children are entitled to education at a public school, which means that the state has to provide schooling facilities. On the other hand, children are also obliged to go to school for 12 years, during which time they receive elementary and secondary education. The term **K-12** is used to describe a child's 12 years of schooling, from kindergarten with preschool programme to the 12th form or grade. **Elementary education** starts in kindergarten and goes on to the 8th grade. It is followed by **secondary education**, at a secondary school or high school, which traditionally comprises grades nine to twelve. The American educational system has always been different from public school systems in Europe. In Germany, primary schools teach all children the basic skills in four years. German children then go on to different schools – Hauptschule, Realschule or Gymnasium –, depending on their abilities and future goals. In contrast, in America there are no separate educational systems, the United States provides one system which is open to everyone. As in comprehensive schools students take different courses in the same buildings according to their talents and capabilities.

Although compulsory schooling usually begins when a child is 6 years old, 60 per cent of American children between the ages of 3 and 5 receive an earlier education. In the formative years before children reach school age, they have already developed an enormous curiosity and have learnt much about their home and their surroundings. To satisfy and encourage their drive for learning, **preschools** such as nursery schools, day schools or day cares and **kindergartens** have been organized. Kindergartens were introduced into the United States by German immigrants. Margarethe Schurz, wife of the German-born reformer and politician Carl Schurz opened the first kindergarten in Wisconsin in 1856. Today kindergartens and day schools in America's cities and communities are normally run by churches or other institutions which are independent of local school systems.

Primary education begins when American children are 6 and start their first class or first grade. School days are from Monday to Friday, usually beginning at 8 o'clock in the morning and lasting till 3 o'clock in the afternoon. Four basic subject areas are included in virtually all elementary schools in the United States: language arts (reading, writing, spelling, and related language skills), mathematics, science, and social science (usually history and geography). Physical education, music and art are also taught. The first aim is to teach "the three R's" – reading, writing, arithmetic. In spring 2000, the US Department of Education set as a goal for primary schools that every 8-year-old should be able to read.

Secondary education at high school comprises four years. It begins between grade 7 and 9 (depending on the state's regulations) and ends with graduation upon completion of the 12th grade or year. Some school districts divide secondary school into lower and upper sections, called junior and senior high school. The divide is usually around 10th or 11th grade. In most high schools the basic courses that are offered are English, science, mathematics, foreign languages, and history. Apart from this core curriculum, secondary schools, following a college tradition, offer a number of courses which are not required, the so-called "electives". These courses include performing arts, driver's education, cooking, and "shop" (use of tools, carpentry, and repair of machinery) for example and are very popular with students. In the last 20 years the number of electives has increased considerably. This has pleased students, but many parents and educators believe that this practice is the primary reason for the slow but steady decline in academic standards. The average scores of American students on standardized tests of mathematics, reading, and science are lower than they were 20 years ago. Some experts blame television which, they say, is producing mediocre programmes. Others argue that teachers are paid too little, with the result that good ones give up teaching, leaving it in the hands of less qualified staff who set their students easy tests so that all of them pass their exams and get a diploma. In spite of a general downward trend in performance, over 70 per cent of high school students complete school with an earned secondary diploma each year. The US education system does not conduct nationwide, official examinations at different levels as in Britain or Germany. Nevertheless, students have to take a wide variety of tests at all educational levels to assess and evaluate their academic progress. Apart from examinations in class, there are also tests in laboratory work and supervised practical or field experiences. Homework, too, is evaluated on a regular basis. When students complete an academic term, they are given their marks, or grades, in each subject they studied as well as a final grade.

Higher Education (Post-school education)

About two-thirds of high school graduates continue in postsecondary education at colleges or universities, with the majority enrolling in bachelor's degree programmes. Regular colleges and universities are largely four-year institutions leading to a **B.A. (Bachelor of Arts)** or **B.S. (Bachelor of Science)**. Other high school leavers choose vocational training schemes which provide direct work-related programmes in skills such as secretarial training, auto mechanics, etc. or go to community or junior colleges – which offer **Associate Degrees** after two years. Since the 1960s it has become easier for students to start college or university because many of these institutions have modified their formerly rigorous admissions policies and also accept less gifted students. However, American politicians like to believe that in the United States education is the great equalizer moulding generations of adolescents into American citizens. The American ideal of equal opportunities for all looks different when you look beneath the surface. This is already evident when children first go to school. Children from rich upper-class or upper-middle-class families go to elite prep schools preparing their students for entry to the elite universities. But the disparities become even more obvious at **postsecondary level**. The great divider is the costs. Postsecondary education is not free – it is rather expensive, and is getting more so every year. In 1997 the average cost of postsecondary education for one academic year was between $ 5,000 at a public community college to $ 19,000 at a private university. Specially gifted students may qualify for grants or scholarships from public and private sources, but the majority have to pay for the cost themselves. Obviously, students from richer families can go to better universities. The most prestigious and most expensive are in the north-eastern part of the United States and are traditionally referred as "**Ivy League**": Harvard (established 1636), Yale (1701), Pennsylvania (1740), Princeton (1746), Columbia (1754), Brown (1764), Dartmouth (1769), and Cornell (1865). All institutions of higher education compete with one another for research and foundation grants and public prestige. The reputation of some colleges and universities derives from their athletic programme and top sportsmen they have enrolled.

A recent development in postsecondary education is "**Learning online**", a system similar to Britain's **Open University** courses or Germany's Fernstudium. Adult learners can complete university classes over the Internet, sitting at home in front of their computers. More than 2 million students are expected to be enrolled in on-line learning courses by 2002.

US Schools in Crisis

School Problems Today

In 1955 the Hollywood film *Blackboard Jungle* shocked cinema goers, because of its drastic scenes of violence in an American metropolitan school. Numerous protests were raised against the screening of the film because it was feared that its showing would provoke even more violence. 40 years later, the 1996 movie *Dangerous Minds*, starring Michelle Pfeiffer, showed a woman teacher of English struggling extremely hard to teach a class of tough, frustrated and aggressive teenagers. There were no protests against the film, although little seems to have changed at America's schools over the last 40 years. Both films are based on the experiences of two teachers and mirror the concern of many Americans that education is in a crisis. The situation is especially desperate in inner-city areas where institutions lack money and staff to cope with increasingly hostile, rough and disinterested students. Almost every day newspaper and television reports about **shootings** in American schools provide proof for the disturbing picture.

In 1998 four girls and a teacher were shot to death and ten people wounded when two boys, 11 and 13, opened fire at their school in Jonesboro, Arkansas. In Littleton, Denver, two teenage murderers killed 15 pupils at their high school and injured many others. Massacres at American schools claimed 30 lives and scores of wounded in the school year 1998–1999. It is not surprising then that safety in schools is widely discussed today and that all schools are stepping up their security precautions. It is common practice that visitors have to sign forms and get visitor's stickers, pupils are not allowed out of their classroom without a pass, staff members patrol buildings regularly, and the whole school area, especially changing rooms and cloakrooms are being surveyed by closed circuit television.

Another problem concerning American schools is the high number of dropouts. It is estimated that every year nearly 5 per cent of American students leave school without taking final exams. This is especially disturbing because **dropouts** are more likely to be out of work and involved in crime and drugs. Most of the students who quit school have a long record of **truancy.** Schools and local authorities have resorted to different measures to enforce school attendance. In some areas truants may have their driver's licence – acquired normally at the age of 16 – suspended and are required to do community service, in others volunteers are sent round to the homes of absent students. In some communities truants under 16 cannot get a work permit, in Washington parents are fined if their children do not turn up at school. Many cities have imposed special laws, called daytime curfews, which authorize police to question and take into custody youngsters who are met in the streets during school hours. Offenders must then appear in juvenile traffic court accompanied by a parent. These curfews were first introduced as night curfews in the 1990s to reduce juvenile crime in large cities. Young people up to 16 had to be off the streets after a certain hour each night. As with violence, the problem of truancy cannot be solved with police measures alone. Truancy is usually a sign that the child has difficulties at home – and the roots of this problem lie in the profound social change in the family structure today. Increasingly, both parents are working and there are growing numbers of single-parent households, so that more often than not are young children left on their own. Parents have to take their responsibilities in bringing up children much more seriously.

School Desegregation and Racial Integration

In 1954 the **Supreme Court** took one of the most important decision in the history of the United States concerning racial relations. The court's ruling put an end to the "**separate but equal**"-doctrine that had been established since 1886 in the case Plessy v. Ferguson. The "separate but equal" policy permitted racial separation of public facilities including schools. Consequently white schools all over the country did not accept black children. In the South, and in many other states as well, black children were especially disadvantaged not enjoying the same chances as white children because the authorities spent much less money on schools for blacks than on schools for whites. In 1950, the father of a black child took the education authorities of Kansas, Texas, to court because he wanted to achieve equal opportunities for all children. Other families also appealed to the court and after hearing a number of school-segregation cases, the Supreme Court finally decided unanimously in 1954 that segregation was against the US constitution. The court overthrew the ruling of 1886 concluded "that in the field of public education the doctrine of 'separate but equal' has no place. Separate educational facilities are inherently unequal." The opinion spurred the **Civil Rights Movement** and brought about fundamental changes in race relations across America.

Following the court's ruling to desegregate schools the government immediately adopted the policy of "**busing**" to promote racial integration. Children from black families were taken by bus from disadvantaged urban areas to schools in predominantly white areas – and vice versa, white children were bussed into black neighbourhoods. This measure of forced integration was never popular and after widespread opposition from whites and, to a lesser extent blacks as well, the policy was eventually abandoned. Many sociologist believe that the problem of racial integration today is even more complex and difficult to solve than in the 1960s and early 1970s. Then the problem of racial segregation was a problem which still concerned mainly two ethnic groups, blacks and whites. Today the issues of diversity are much more complicated due to the dramatic growth in the **Latino** and the **Asian-American population**. Half the recent population growth in the US has been in just three states – in Florida, Texas and California. The majority of the growth in those areas, and in school enrolments particularly, is Latino. People from Spanish-speaking countries (Cuba,

Busing programs were introduced to promote integration of black and white children at school.

Mexico, San Salvador) settle in the Southern and Western states of the USA and form their own communities. Living together they retain their culture and traditions by keeping their own language. In some parts of Miami and Los Angeles tourists can make themselves understood today if they speak Spanish.

Bilingual Education

More than 5 million Americans do not speak English well and 2 million do not speak it at all. There is also an increasing number of Hispanic-Americans who speak "Spanglish", a mixture of English and Spanish with few rules and many variations. In their conversations speakers use the word that comes first to their mind – be it Spanish or English ("Hasta soon ..."). Linguists call this mix of two languages "code-mixing". Some Hispanics use this new type of language, because they find it too difficult to switch over to English completely, others want to keep their Spanish heritage.

In order to reach their Hispanic voters during election campaigns, Republican and Democratic candidates have some of their political commercials broadcast in Spanish. During his presidency Bill Clinton had a wide range of government documents translated into Spanish, so that Latinos could read and understand vital government information on education and health – particularly on immunization, adoption and parenthood. In 1974 a Supreme Court ruling ordered schools to provide extra help to pupils whose English was deficient. Following this decision states with high immigration rates introduced the system of "**Bilingual Education**". In California – home of half the nation's immigrants – and a number of other states "Bilingual Education" became compulsory. Since then students who were considered "**limited English proficient**" have been taught both in English and in their mother tongue Spanish. It was hoped that by using this method children would overcome their language problem at school and integration could be facilitated. However, in recent years the bilingual approach has met with increased criticism. Numerous initiatives were started demanding to replace the bilingual programmes with "**English-immersion**" **classes** – to place immigrants in English-only classes where "they either swim or sink", as one teacher put it. Opponents argued bilingual classes were too expensive and did not work. In their view the best way to learn English quickly would be to learn it with English peers – children of the same age group.

As immigration, both legal and illegal, brought new floods of foreigners into the United States, anti-immigrant sentiment grew and campaigns to make English the nation's official language gathered strength. Supporters of a lobby group called "US English" expressed their fear that the American ideal of the melting pot would come to an end. A particularly worrying issue in this context is the recent discussion of the future status of **Puerto Rico.** Since 1952 the island has been a US commonwealth, which means it enjoys political autonomy but is under the direct authority of the US Congress. The advocates of "US English" predict long-term negative consequences for the United States should the Puerto Ricans vote for US statehood and be admitted into the Union. Not only is Puerto Rico a very poor country with a high unemployment rate, but above all its people speak Spanish. According to "US English" members, a Spanish-speaking state in the Union would eventually erode the American culture. To avoid this from happening, immigrants should be taught English, because only by learning the language would they be able to integrate into the American society. A multi-millionaire sponsored an initiative to alter California's laws and eliminate bilingual education. In a referendum held in 1998, Californians voted for the adoption of the amendment, known as **Proposition 227**. This means that all students in public schools must be taught primarily in English unless their parents request otherwise. Critics say that the abolition of bilingual education will actually lead to fewer children learning English and many children will fall further behind in their studies or leave school without any qualification. Today about 7 per cent of students are not proficient in English, in California it is 25 per cent. Most of them are in elementary grades and come from Spanish-speaking families. The abolition of bilingual education classes in California will also have implications for the way English is taught throughout the United States.

The Search for Alternatives: Private Schools and Home Schooling

Many parents, teacher and politicians complain about the low academic standard at American schools. Politicians of both parties, Republicans and Democrats, have made numerous efforts to raise student achievement and improve school standards, for example by advocating the establishment of nationwide tests. Months after becoming president in 1989, Republican George Bush called a meeting of the nation's 50 governors, all of whom agreed in a declaration that it was necessary to improve the quality of education. During Democrat Bill Clinton's presidency the US Congress passed the **Goals 2000: Educate America Act** – a legislation which gave states government aid to help them devise their own academic standards. In 1994 and in 1996 two education summits were called, where governors reaffirmed their commitment to public education. However, due to the decentralised organisation of the US education system the federal government cannot enforce a change. Many schools adopt the recommendations of the Department of Education and tighten their requirements, other do not or cannot. In poor neighbourhoods and ghettos, where school boards can only draw on rather limited funds to equip their institutions, the situation is getting worse. Incidents of violence, drug dealing, overcrowding and under-qualified teachers make parents look for a way out of the dilemma to find better ways of educating and qualifying their children. They make use of the fact that although school attendance is compulsory in the United States it need not be at a public school. The alternatives parents have found are **home schooling** and **private** or **charter schools**.

Schools in run-down inner-city areas lack money and staff to improve the chances for the disadvantaged children living there.

Whereas public schools do not charge for tuition, parents who send their children to private schools or have decided on home schooling have to bear the tuition cost themselves. Despite this disadvantage over 12 per cent of all school children today are either being tutored at home or enrolled in private schools. Private schools run by religious groups are called **parochial schools**. The largest systems are operated by the **Roman Catholic** and **Lutheran denominations**, and there is also a great number of **Jewish schools**. Within parochial school education, the most rapid expansion is within the Muslim community, which now has about 200 schools across the United States. Other private schools and colleges are sponsored by individuals, by foundations or firms. In 1971 many private schools ran into financial difficulties when the Supreme Court decided that direct state aid to non-public elementary and secondary schools was against the constitution. This ruling also increased problems for the public school system, because when many Roman Catholic had to close, the students of these schools had to be integrated into the **public school system**. In 1984 parents of children at private schools suffered another blow. Congress rejected a plan to grant them tax relief for having their children tutored in private schools. All of this makes private schools a viable but expensive alternative.

A recent development within the American system of education are the so-called "**charter schools**", which were first established in Minnesota in the early 1990s. Charter schools use public funds, but they are run with more freedom and flexibility than typical public schools. The US government, Congress and a number of states such as Michigan and Arizona support this type of school, hoping that students' performance will be much better than in public schools. Furthermore, it is believed that the funding of the charter school system will do away with the long-standing inequality between schools in cities and in the country, caused by **property tax funding**. As to the teaching, supporters say charter schools allow innovative teachers to try new ideas, especially because these institutions are free to create their own curriculum and tend to be small. On the other hand, critics argue that running and funding these schools is a waste of money which the public school system could use better and more effectively. They add that there is little evidence that charter schools improve student achievement in the long run.

An increasing number of families are taking the education of their children into their own hands. The movement which is becoming more popular is called "**home schooling**" and means that school-aged children are being taught by their parents at home. It is estimated that over two million students in the United States are educated in this way. Home schooling replaces full-time attendance at a school, but some children enrol part time at a campus-based school or share instruction with other families. The reasons why parents turn their backs on the public education system are many-fold. Some are worried about the low academic standards at the schools in their area and are convinced that their children will profit from intensive home schooling. Religious belief is also an important factor. Many Muslims for example educate their children at home because they believe that teaching their children an Islamic way of life can only be done at home. Other parents do not want to send their children to chaotic, loud and overcrowded 'factory schools', which they regard as unable to deal with both learning-disabled and highly gifted children. Others put high emphasis on teaching moral and ethical behaviour, which, in their view, is neglected at public schools. In the **American College Testing Programme** home school students achieved better results than public school students of the same grade. An explanation for this could be the fact that home school children receive the full attention of their "teacher" – and are made to pay attention and do their homework properly.

Home schooling requires a lot of responsibility, time, and devotion to teaching one's offspring and many parents who started it found the task too difficult and eventually gave up. All in all, in the United States parents are free to choose the best school for their children, be it a public school, a private or home school.

Religion

The United States – a Religious Society

Europeans often think that Americans are not religious – the opposite is true: America can be described as one of the most religious societies in the world. There are some 2,000 different denominations and almost 500,000 churches, temples and mosques all over the USA to prove the remarkable religious vitality of the American society.

- American **Protestant** churches have approximately 94 million members, spread across 220 particular denominations including Baptists (Al Gore, Bill Clinton), Methodists (George W. Bush), Lutherans, Anglicans and Episcopalians (who combine Protestant and Roman Catholic traditions) and Quakers.
- Roman **Catholics** are the second largest denomination with some 60 million adherents (John F. Kennedy). Due to Hispanic immigration the number of Catholics is increasing.
- About 3.8 million Americans are **Jews** (an additional 2 million define themselves as primarily culturally or ethnically Jewish).
- An estimated 5 million are **Muslims**; because of the immigration from Islamic countries it is the most rapidly growing religion in the US.

Americans openly express their faith. Students wear T-shirts that promote religion ("Jesus saves"), celebrities such as film stars Richard Gere (Buddhist) and John Travolta (Scientologist) talk frankly about their convictions. A murderess seeks refuge in religious contemplation. "I am going to be face to face with Jesus now," said Karla Faye Tucker, the woman who murdered her husband with a pickaxe in 1983, in her final words before being executed. The governor of the state of Texas, George Bush Jr., rejected Ms Tucker's call for clemency, after he had sought guidance through prayer.

Religion seems to have turned into a commodity on the market. There is currently a growing world of religious rock music; religious radio and television broadcasting have become a major element of contemporary American religion and religious bookstores are an increasing phenomenon. One-third of Americans watch at least one religious television programme a week, and whereas in other western industrialised societies the number of church-goers is on the decline, more Americans attend religious events every week than professional sporting events: Four in ten Americans go regularly to church, synagogue, mosque or the temple. In Britain, only one person in ten identifies with a religion, in the United States seven in ten say they are church members. Despite the religious variety and the enthusiasm with which people profess their belief and show their connection with some faith or congregation critics within and outside the churches ask whether this religiousness is really deeply felt or only superficial. Are Americans religious for social reasons, and is it merely a custom and a tradition for the family to drive to church every Sunday morning? For the outward observers the record of organized religion is impressive, but critics feel less confident when they weigh up the impact of religion in American society and politics (e. g. gun violence, shootings in schools, death penalty in many states) and the great divide between the very rich and very poor.

Separation of Church and State

The first settlers emigrated to the New World primarily because they were looking for a place to practice their faith without being persecuted by the government. Consequently, to avoid any interference from the government in religious matters the authors of the Constitution of the United States saw to it that there was a strict separation between state and church. England served as a warning example which they did not want to follow. The British Sovereign was "**Defender of the Faith**" and head of the Anglican Church, the state church. This close link was established in 1534 when King Henry VIII had separated the English Church from Rome in order to obtain a divorce from his first wife Catherine of Aragon. He had then proclaimed himself "Supreme Head of the Church of England", thus starting a tradition alive until today. When the American colonists drew up their Constitution at the end of the 18th century they had two aims in mind – as far as religion was concerned. First of all, they wished to protect the right of each individual to **free exercise of religion**. The right of free religious worship was not extended to the Native Americans, whose religious practices and traditions were treated with little respect by the white invaders. In the second place the creators of the Constitution wanted to **prohibit the establishment of religion** through the state. Therefore, the First Amendment to the US Constitution reads like this: "Congress shall make no law respecting an establishment of religion, or prohibiting the free exercise thereof ...". The two most influential politicians advocating this double principle were Thomas Jefferson and James Madison. Jefferson had gained fame and respect as the author of the Statutes of Religious Liberty for Virginia, in which he presented himself as a fervent defender of religious freedom. Together with his co-author James Madison, who held similar views on freedom of worship: "The Religion then of every man must be left to the conviction and conscience of every man; and it is the right of every man to exercise it as these may dictate. This right is in its nature an unalienable right." Both men were responsible for the wording of Article VI of the American Constitution which reflects their conviction: "No religious test shall ever be required as a qualification to any office or public trust under the United States." By accepting this principle the representatives at the Constitutional Convention in Philadelphia broke with European tradition and opened public office in the federal government to people of all faiths or none at all. The separation of church and state keeps the government out of religious matters, but it has also practical consequences. The congregations do not receive any financial support from the government, and there are no taxes deducted from people's income as in Germany. There are no religious holidays. For Christians in the United States, Sunday is a religious holiday, but for non-Christians it is the only common-law holiday. Many advocates of the full separation of church and state argue that this system makes the churches more alive, because they are forced to find their own resources in contrast to state-supported churches.

The Statue of Liberty, a present of the people of France to the USA in 1884, has become a symbol of freedom to people all over the world.

Debate about the First Amendment

Although the First Amendment aims at a separation between church and state there are numerous examples that in practice there has often been a connection between politics and religion. From the early days of the colonists to the present day, religions and religious beliefs have played a significant role in the political life of the United States. During the American War of Independence religion offered a guarantee to the average American that the revolution against the mother country England was justified in the sight of God. Later, when the white settlers moved into Indian territory and displaced and killed the native Indians they did this in the "name of God". The newly developed concept of "**Manifest Destiny**" reassured them that it was the Godly mission of the white man to conquer the wilderness and civilize primitive "savages". In his protest song "With God On Our Side" the singer and poet Bob Dylan criticised the self-righteousness of the Americans in believing that all their wars had been fought for a just cause and that the American people had always had "God on their side". Every session of the US Congress begins regularly with a prayer by a minister. When addressing the American public via television every president ends his Message on the State of the Union with the word "God bless you" or "God bless America". At the inauguration ceremony the new president is sworn in and confirms the oath he takes with the formula "So help me God"! These practices are only a formality or a tradition, but there are also religious issues which have caused social conflict and strife.

The controversy over the First Amendment arises from the fact that it has been interpreted in two different ways. Some people see it as the Founding Fathers' provision that the government should stay out of religion completely. The opponents of this view argue that the First Amendment must not be used to make America a religion-free country. A vivid illustration of this difficulty to determine how far government influence can be allowed is the never-ending debate over prayer and religious practices at America's public schools. The most recent example is the argument about prayers before school sports matches. When the school authorities in Santa Fé allowed students in June 2000 to initiate and lead prayers over the public-address system before the football games a parent group opposed this permission and filed a lawsuit arguing that the school district's policy violated the First Amendment by creating a "pervasive religious atmosphere". The argument over public prayer has been put before the US Supreme Court more than once. As early as 1948 the court ruled that allowing religious teachers to come into public schools to give religious instruction violated the First Amendment. In 1980 the court struck down a Kentucky law requiring the posting of the Ten Commandments in all public classrooms. On the other hand, the court did not support aims to make schools religion-free zones. It endorsed a federal law that gave equal access to student groups, including religious groups, to high school premises. Of major importance for the current debate is a decision taken in 1992. The court ruled 5–4 that school-sponsored prayers at graduation and other official school functions violated the First Amendment. The court reaffirmed that the Constitution guarantees that the government cannot coerce anyone to support or participate in religion or its exercise. However, these rulings have made the opposition even stronger in their efforts to campaign against a policy which in their opinion is hostile to religion. Religion, they say, is too important to America's history and heritage to keep it out of the country's schools. Both Al Gore and George W. Bush, the Democrat and Republican candidates in the presidential election 2000, supported student-led prayer because they were convinced that religious values had to be taught at schools. The conflict in Santa Fé angered large parts of the community to such a degree that the two families – one Catholic and one Mormon – who sued the school board had to fear for their lives, and the courts hid their identities. It may never be possible to resolve the apparent inconsistencies of the First Amendment, even scholars of the constitution find it hard to draw a clear line between state interference and religious freedom. It might be said, however, the vast majority of American parents do not want a withdrawal of the church and church symbols from state schools. The compromise could be that religious practices at schools cannot be demanded, but on the other hand, must not be denied.

Religious Diversity

There was another reason for Jefferson and Madison to insist on including the separation of church and state into the Constitution. Not all the Founding Fathers believed in the same God, or in any God at all come to that. The Declaration of Independence refers to a deity, but only in the most general terms – "Nature's God", the "Creator", "Providence". These words were chosen in order not to offend the doubters and deists (who believed that God had designed the universe, then left it to nature to run). Jefferson was a renowned doubter, urging his nephew to "question with boldness even the existence of a God".

There was also a practical reason for the framers of the Constitution and the Bill of Rights to support religious pluralism. In the 18th century many immigrants arrived in the New World because they wanted to be free from government interference in the practice of their religious beliefs. The politicians assembled in Philadelphia realized that it was practically impossible – and politically unwise – to establish one religion for the emerging new nation, because none of the different religious groups was strong enough to dominate the others. This means that the religious diversity, which we observe in the United States today, has its roots in the history of immigration to the New World. Through the centuries the religious landscape of America expanded greatly. In the beginning, in the 17th century, Protestantism in various forms was the dominant religion. Today more than 2,000 religious groups can be found in the United States living side by side.

Religious Groups

Protestants

The first settlers who came to North America were Puritans and Calvinists who were looking for a place where they could practice their faith without being persecuted by the government. These groups had developed in the wake of the Reformation in the 16th century. Because of the Protestant tendency of their religious belief the Separatist Puritans were regarded as outsiders, as non-conformists, by the established state church, the Church of England and were not allowed to practise their religion freely. The dissenters left England and first moved to Holland where they found temporary asylum. They formed the Separatist congregation at Leiden, but eventually left the Old World because they had obtained permission by the Virginia Company to settle in America and set sail across the Atlantic. The **Puritans**, who were later known as **Pilgrim Fathers**, hired the ship Mayflower, a 12-year-old vessel which had been used in the wine trade, and left England on September 16, 1620. The historic voyage took 65 days, during which two of the 102 passengers died. The colonists had been granted territory in Virginia, but the Mayflower came off course and instead of landing in Virginia the ship dropped anchor at Provincetown (Massachusetts) on November 21, 1620. 41 men signed the so-called **Mayflower Compact**, which became the basis of government in the Plymouth Colony, and elected John Carver their first governor.

Since the days of the Pilgrims many people have emigrated to the American Colonies in search of freedom of worship.

In the 18th century America became a religious refuge for many Protestant communities which eventually gave the new American nation a mainly Protestant face. Today Protestantism is still the dominant creed with 94 million adherents. After the Pilgrims – the term was first used by William Bradford to describe the **Leiden Separatists** – more and more followers of different religious groups arrived in the North American colonies. Anglicans settled in the South, and Puritans in New England. Although the majority of the sects had come in flight from religious persecution in their homelands, they did not show the tolerance they themselves had searched for towards other religious refugees. People with diverging theological views were not always accepted by the original Pilgrims and consequently established new colonies of their own in which they enjoyed religious liberty. New England became the home of various Puritan groups, Pennsylvania and New York had substantial numbers of Lutherans, minor German Protestant groups, and members of the Society of Friends or Quakers. Early Virginia was largely identified with Baptists and Methodists. However, in the course of time, the religious groups became more tolerant and began to learn to live together. The Constitution eventually contributed to settling and avoiding sectarian conflicts by guaranteeing religious freedom for all Americans.

Very soon different schools within the Protestant movement developed. On the one hand, there were the liberal Protestants who were reading and interpreting the Bible in a new way. They questioned the validity of biblical miracles, traditional beliefs about the authorship of biblical books and sought a lessening of doctrine. Today this branch is referred to as "mainstream Protestantism". On the other hand there were – and still are – the conservatives, often called "evangelicals" because of their enthusiasm for the gospels of the New Testament. They believed that departures from the exact truth of the Bible were unjustified. The largest Protestant groups include the **Baptists** (27 million followers), **Methodists** (9.2 million), **Lutherans** (8 million), **Episcopalians** (2.8 million), **Congregationalists** and **Quakers**.

Baptists

The Baptist Church first appeared in England and Wales in the early 17th century. The movement has almost 35 million followers worldwide and is particularly strong in the United States. The first Baptist church in the New World was established in 1639, at Providence, Rhode Island by Roger Williams, an English colonist who refused to associate himself with the Anglican Puritans. The name of the community derives from its most noted practice of baptism of adults by immersion. Baptists believe that only adults are prepared to make a personal confession of faith in Jesus Christ. In the late 18th and 19th centuries the Baptist church found an increasing number of followers in the USA, especially among the Southern black population. Black Baptist churches, and their ministers, played an important role in the civil rights movement of the 1960s, led by Martin Luther King. The **Baptist World Alliance** was formed in 1905. In Baptist church services the emphasis lies on Bible reading and preaching. Baptists strongly believe in the Bible and interpret the scripture literally. In 1998 a statement of delegates of the strong and influential **Southern Baptist Convention** – a congregation of almost 16 million adherents – received wide media coverage. In their resolution on the family the Baptists delegates included their belief that a wife should "submit herself graciously" to her husband. Whereas most media criticised the statement, it was welcomed by church members who wanted their church to give them and the society as a whole stronger moral guidelines. Vice-president Al Gore, Democrat runner for the presidency in 2000, and his family attend New Salem Missionary Baptist Church in Carthage, Tennessee.

Methodists

It is estimated that there are about 26 million **Methodists** world-wide today, the largest single group is the United Methodist Church in the United States with about 9 million members. The Methodist movement was started in England by the Wesley brothers, John and Charles Wesley, and George Whitefield in the 18th-century who organized small "societies" within the Church of England for Bible study, prayer, and preaching. The **Wesleyan Movement**, as it was first called, soon spread worldwide because the Wesleys and their associate Whitefield travelled widely, preaching to large and enthusiastic crowds of working people. After John Wesley's death in 1791 the Methodists separated from the Church of England, and in 1843 the **Wesleyan Methodist Church of America** was started. The group played a major role in the fight against slavery: Three large black Methodist churches were also organized in protest against racial prejudice. Republican George W. Bush, elected President in 2000, is a member of the Methodist church.

Catholics

The number of Roman Catholics in the USA increased in the 19th century when hundreds of thousands of Irish people were driven from their homeland by the Great Famine. Potato crop failures in Ireland had forced them to leave their homes, so that by the time of the Civil War (1861–1865) over one million Irish Catholics had come to the United States. As they were not usually welcomed by the Protestant majority the Catholics started their own schools in which the teaching of Catholic doctrines and morality was given great priority. Because of their discipline and quality of education these private schools eventually attracted a growing number of non-Catholic students. Until today they have retained their prestige and are still popular places of instruction, although they do not receive public funds and are financed by tuition fees paid by parents. In recent years Catholic parents sought financial assistance from the state for maintaining their separate educational system, reasoning that they saved the government money by sending their children to private schools.

However, the Supreme Court ruled that if the state supported religious schools this would violate the **First Amendment**. Governmental subsidies were therefore unconstitutional.

Prejudices against Catholics have had a long tradition in the United States. Anti-Catholic feelings were so deep-rooted that they could still be observed more than a hundred years after the first waves of immigration of Irish Catholics. In 1960 some Americans opposed the presidential candidate of the Democratic Party, John F. Kennedy, because he was a Catholic, arguing, if elected, Kennedy would receive his orders from the Pope in Rome. In spite of these absurd accusations Kennedy won the presidency, but he has remained the only Catholic American president to date.

Jews

Similarly to Catholics, Jews were a small minority in the first years of the American republic. Most Jews came from Germany and belonged to the Reform movement, a liberal branch of Judaism which had modified the old doctrines and adjusted to modern life. Therefore they were readily accepted into society when they first arrived in the United States and anti-Semitism was not a big problem before the Civil War. However, the situation changed and anti-Semitism developed when the immigration waves of the 19th century brought an ever larger number of orthodox Jews from Russia and Poland to the United States. These newcomers who strictly observed the traditions (dress, celebrations) and laws (diets) of Judaism and preferred to live closely together in certain quarters of the cities were often regarded as outsiders. Today more Jews live in the United States than in any other country, including Israel. Many came between 1935 and 1945 from Germany to escape from Nazi persecution, but since 1950 most Jews have come from the Middle East and Eastern European countries. Not all of them kept to the traditional rites and practices which were looked upon as rather strange by many Americans, but adopted a nonreligious and more open position. The fact that these less orthodox believers regarded themselves simply as ethnically Jewish helped to increase an atmosphere of tolerance. Intermarriages between Christians and Jews further promoted integration. People of Jewish faith have made important contributions in all walks of American life, especially in the fields of politics, finance and banking (Wall Street), art, the press, science and in the entertainment industry. Famous Jewish Americans are writers Saul Bellow and Arthur Miller, composers George Gershwin, Leonard Bernstein, film producers Louis B. Mayer and Samuel Goldwyn, comedians Jack Benny and the Marx Brothers, film stars Goldie Hawn, Bette Midler, Charlton Heston, Dustin Hoffman and

Orthodox Jews preparing for the traditional Hebrew festival Sukkot, which lasts seven days in September and October.

Michael Douglas, singers Barbra Streisand and Carly Simon. Many Jewish immigrants moved rapidly into the professions and into American universities, where they became intellectual leaders. Nobel laureates are Albert Einstein, Milton Friedman and Henry Kissinger.

Islamic faith

Although Protestants, Catholics and Jews are different in many ways they have one thing in common: they all come from a Judeo-Christian cultural and historical background. Immigration to the US in the 19th and 20th centuries changed the mix of religious groups considerably, but America's overall heritage remained primarily European. This situation changed in the mid-1960s with the revision of the immigration laws, when more non-European immigrants were admitted to the United States. New groups from Asia, Latin America and the Middle East brought their cultural and religious values and contributed significantly to the growth of the Islamic faith, which today has about 5 million adherents. The number of mosques in the United States has doubled in the last 15 years to 1250 mosques and Islamic centres. Buddhism and Hinduism are also growing with the arrival of immigrants from India, Pakistan and Bangladesh. Seeking an alternative to their "slave" identities, many African Americans converted to the Islamic faith as they believed that many of the original slaves would likely have been Muslim. In 1930 Wallace D. Fard founded the separatist movement Nation of Islam which was later led by Elijah Muhammad and became known as **Black Muslims** – at different times also referred to as the **American Muslim Mission** and the **World Community of Islam in the West**. Members of the movement demanded a separate state for blacks and avoided contact with whites. As outward proof of their new identity they adopted Muslim names. After joining the Black Muslims the American boxer Cassius Marcellus Clay gave up his original "slave name" and assumed the name Muhammad Ali. He also refused to be drafted to the US army arguing that he was a Black Muslim minister and therefore a conscientious objector. In 1978 Muhammad Ali became the first boxer to win the world heavyweight championship title three times.

One of the best-known Black Muslim ministers, who had converted while he was in prison in 1947, was Malcolm X. When the movement turned more militant in the 1960s, Malcolm X broke with the group and was assassinated in 1965. In 2000, Louis Farrakhan, the leader of a radical splinter group of the Muslim movement which call themselves by the original name **Nation of Islam**, admitted he "may have been complicit in words" in the 1965 assassination of rival leader Malcolm X. Farrakhan's splinter group has retained the separatist principles of the early days of the Muslim movement and his racial comments and frequent anti-Semitic attacks have caused wide-spread debate, disagreement and fury. The majority of the Black Muslims, however, today repudiate their early separatism and have adopted orthodox Muslim beliefs.

Mormons

America has been a fertile ground for new religions. The Mormon and **Christian Science Churches** are perhaps the best-known of the faiths that have sprung up on American soil. About 7.7 million people in the United States are members of the **Mormons** or **Latter-day Saints**. In 1830 Joseph Smith founded the Church. He claimed having had visions of God in which he was told to establish the restored Christian church. The Angel **Moroni**, one of the heavenly messengers, Smith maintained, directed him to some golden plates, inscribed in a hieroglyphic language, which he translated. His translation is the **Book of Mormon**, which describes the history, wars, and religious beliefs of a group of people (c. 600 BC–AD 421) who migrated from Jerusalem to America – long before Christopher Columbus discovered America. Smith attracted a small group of followers who moved to northern Missouri and then to Illinois. The Mormons met with opposition and were persecuted because Smith had introduced **polygamy** into Mormonism. On June 27, 1844, an armed mob assassinated Smith, and Brigham Young became his successor. In 1846 Young organized and directed the heroic march from Illinois across the plains and mountains to the Great Salt Basin in Utah. After Congress had passed anti-bigamy laws (1862 and 1882) and the Supreme Court had ruled that religious freedom did not allow the practice of polygamy, the Mormons discarded plural marriage. Like Baptists, Mormons are baptized by immersion at age eight or older. Since they believe in baptism for the dead, members may undergo baptismal rites on behalf of their ancestors. One of the main aims of the church is missionary work. The Mormons have no professional clergy, therefore all members are encouraged to perform religious service. More than 37,000 young men and women devote two years of their lives to working as missionaries. The church lays great importance on family solidarity, to this end a weekly family evening of religious instruction and entertainment is organized. The abstention from tea, coffee, alcohol, and tobacco is laid down in a code of health, called "**Word of Wisdom**". Mormons oppose the Equal Rights Amendment because in their view the equality of the sexes upsets family life.

Christian Science

Christian Science, which today has about 3,000 branch churches, societies, and college organizations in more than 50 countries, was founded by Mary Baker Eddy in 1879 in Boston as the **Church of Jesus Christ**, Scientist. The central belief is that God is the only reality, and the material world, with all its suffering, strife, and death, is unreal. It is considered to be a misunderstanding or deformed view of the divine universe. Illnesses are also regarded as delusions of the human mind and consequently can be healed by praying for the right understanding. Members of the church refuse to resort to medical or other material means to cure diseases and rely on divine law in times of sickness. Christian Science parents who claim the right to withhold medical treatment from their children have been convicted of criminal negligence. Mary Eddy formulated the rules of the group in the **Manual of the Mother Church** (1895). The rules say that Sunday services are to consist mainly of readings from the Bible and the textbook of Christian Science, which was also written by Mary Baker Eddy. The church has no ordained clergy, and readers, both men and women, are elected from the membership to perform the services. The highly respected **Christian Science Monitor** (founded in 1908) is a general daily newspaper, which is published by the Christian Science Publishing Society, but carries little about the doctrines of Christian Science church.

Other Churches

The religious landscape in the United States is so diverse, due to the extraordinary tolerance which Americans have always shown towards people of different beliefs and convictions. "Live and let live" has been the motto since the republic was first founded and thus the US has provided a home for many small sects from overseas. In the 18th century a conservative Protestant group, the **Mennonites**, fled from persecution in Europe and settled in Pennsylvania. People called them **Amish** after their Swiss bishop Jakob Amman. The members of the Amish communities live simple lives, wear plain clothes and reject the usage of modern machinery and technology. The Hollywood film "Witness" with Harrison Ford made the group known all over the world and every year thousands of tourists visit the Amish communities in Pennsylvania and neighbouring states. Other churches with a significant membership are the Jehovah's Witnesses, the Seventh-Day Adventists and the **Disciples of Christ**. In 1954 L. Ron Hubbard founded **Scientology**, recognized as a church in the US but not in Germany because of some of its radical measures of mind control and the fact that members are expected to contribute large sums of money.

The Amish came to America early in the 18th century and until today run and work their farms without any machines and modern agricultural methods. Amish men wear broad-brimmed black hats, women wear bonnets and long full dresses with capes.

Sects and Cults

The great tolerance in religious matters has given rise to a number of groups with extremist or esoteric beliefs, many of which tend to glorify a founding figure, like for example **Bhagwan Rajneesh** in Oregon in the 1970s. Other sects are the **Moonies**, known for their mass weddings, and the **Hare Krishnas** which appeal especially to young people in search of answer to the problems in a confusing modern world. Most Americans regard these cults as rather bizarre, but as long as their members abide by the law they are free to exercise their "religion". On the other hand, there have always been groups whose eccentric leaders have had a detrimental influence on their followers. In 1970 Charles Manson, who thought of himself as Christ, ordered members of his cult to commit nine cold-blooded ritual murders. One of the persons killed was the pregnant wife of the film director Roman Polanski. A mass suicide of 900 brainwashed followers of a religious commune occurred in 1978. A massacre took place at a farm owned by the **Branch Davidian** religious sect near Waco in Texas in 1993. For 51 days agents of the FBI and the Bureau of Alcohol, Tobacco and Firearms laid siege on the sect's heavily fortified compound because they wanted to arrest cult leader David Koresh on weapons charges. In the end eighty-six people were shot or burned to death and the farm was destroyed completely. Great parts of the press and the public later criticized the FBI, arguing that an inflammable form of teargas had been used in the assault. The Department of Justice, however, defended the actions of the agents.

Religious Movements and the Conservative Right

The Great Awakening

America has seen several religious revival movements which cut across denominational lines. Inspired by their evangelical fervour revivalists travelled across the continent with their message of salvation through Christ alone, evoking a deeply personal and emotional response in thousands of Americans. In the middle of the 18th and at the beginning of the 19th century two waves swept through the states: the **First** and the **Second Great Awakening**. The most fervent preachers of this evangelist movement were the **Methodists** and **Baptists**. Around 1740 several Protestant denominations united in an effort to revive interest in religion. They had noticed that in the American colonies people had developed a sense of self-righteousness which had caused them to neglect their search of God and religious practices. The most famous preacher who sought to inspire the communities with new enthusiasm was the English travelling preacher George Whitefield, who became the leader of Calvinistic Methodism. Whitefield stressed the importance of vital religious experience as the cornerstone of effective religious life. However, more conservative parsons did not welcome the confusion brought about by the **Great Awakening**, arguing that emotions destroyed man's rational control of his destiny. A revival of the movement, called the Second Great Awakening, occurred in the early 19th century with the same purpose of revitalizing the churches spiritually. New organisation were formed, such as the American Bible Society and the American Sunday School Union, to carry God's word into the outlying parts of the expanding new nation. Missionaries travelled into the West to encourage the settlers to read the Bible, build churches, attend Sunday church services in order to advance morality and political stability – and to convert the native American Indians.

Dwight Lyman Moody

The most noted travelling evangelist of the late 19th century was Dwight Lyman Moody, who was born on a small New England farm in Northfield, Massachusetts, in 1837. Moody came from a very poor family – his father died when he was four and his mother had to provide for her seven children. At 16 the young boy left home and first worked in shoe shops in Boston and Chicago. Knowing what it was like to be poor, Moody tried to help homeless children in a run-down area on Chicago's north side by setting up a small Sunday school in an abandoned freight car. He did not only preach the gospel, he also taught the children of poor immigrants the English language and proper behaviour. In order to attract children to his Sunday school Moody offered prizes, free pony rides, picnics and promised free suits at Christmas for those boys who attended church service regularly. In a very short time Moody's Sunday School became the largest in town, reaching some 1,500 children weekly. Wealthy businessmen looked upon Moody's work with sympathy and supported him with donations. In 1863 he started preaching to adults on Sunday evenings, which was the beginning of what became known as the **Moody Memorial Church**. Moody's career took a decisive turn in 1870 when he met Ira A. Sankey, a post office worker from Pennsylvania, who in his free time performed as a musician and singer at church services. Moody invited Sankey to join him as a chorister in Chicago, and in 1871 both men started their revival campaigns to major American and British cities. For almost 20 years the team of Moody and Sankey moved their revivals from one major urban centre to the next, preaching to millions and converting thousands. The exceptional success which they achieved was based on the fact that Moody organized his tours efficiently like a business. He used the press to advertise his rallies, made his services entertaining, with Sankey's music representing a major ingredient, and avoided complicated theological teaching. Moody retired in 1892 and died seven years later.

Evangelists and the Electronic Church

Revivalist Dwight Lyman Moody laid the basis for the **evangelists** of today. Their aims are the same, but their methods are different. Like their forerunners the evangelists of today lay great emphasis on the believer's personal relationship with Jesus Christ and his or her commitment to the demands of the New Testament. In their preaching they call on the hearer to confess his sin and believe in Christ's forgiveness. They aim at promoting the reading of the Bible and try to convert people to Christian belief. Instead of travelling the country, like the 19th century revivalists, the preachers of today make use of the most advanced technologies of information, radio, television and the Internet. This is why they are called "preachers of the Electronic Church". The most prominent American evangelist of the 20th century and head of an enormous organisation devoted to the spread of the Bible is Billy Graham, who, to a large extent, followed the footsteps of the revivalists of the 19th century. Graham revived the fundamentalist religious movement of the late 19th century and became the spokesman for conservative Protestants in the United States.

Billy Graham

William Franklin Graham gained a worldwide reputation for his charismatic preaching and evangelistic crusades. He was born on a farm in Charlotte, N.C., in 1918 and endured dire poverty. After attending the famous Wheaton College, near Chicago, he entered the ministry as pastor of the First Baptist Church of Western Springs, Illinois, became a leader in the **Youth for Christ movement** and organized a revival team in 1947. Graham studied the methods of evangelists Homer Rodeheaver and Donald G. Barnhouse and quickly became an expert in all the practical techniques of his work as evangelist. He was not interested in complicated theological concepts and did not hesitate to use methods of modern publicity and public relation, from organising promotional material to leading a Motorcade for Christ. Graham's young team achieved the first big success in 1949, when several prominent Hollywood personalities were converted to Christianity. The **Billy Graham Evangelistic Association** was founded in 1950 to promote crusades, develop radio and television programmes and produce films. Graham was readily accepted in the circles of high society – in 1969, he prayed at the inauguration of President Richard Nixon – and met all important politicians, Kings and Queens and hundreds of celebrities. He also served some American presidents as advisor. In spite of his world-wide success – in South Korea he once preached to a million people – Billy Graham always thought of himself first and foremost as "an ambassador of the King of Kings and the Lord of Hosts". In his autobiography the evangelist wondered about his success, asking God, "Why me, Lord? Why did You choose a farm boy from North Carolina to preach to so many people, to have such a wonderful team of associates, and to have a part in what You were doing in the latter half of the 20th century?"

TV Evangelists and the Rise of the Conservative Right

Observers from Europe are always fascinated and sometimes puzzled in which way the revival movement has used the modern means of communication to spread the word of God. Every Sunday preachers like Pat Robertson, Jerry Falwell and Jimmy Lee Swaggart attract millions of viewers to their TV sermons. Swaggart decided to be a full-time preacher in 1958, launched a radio program in 1969, and within 10 years became the most popular US television preacher. Jerry Falwell formed the **Thomas Road Baptist Church** in 1956 and soon after began radio and television broadcasts of his popular "Old Time Gospel Hour". In 1979 he founded the conservative political organization **Moral**

Majority. Pat Robertson, the son of a United States senator, is Chairman of the Board of the cable network, "The Family Channel" (TFC). The Southern Baptist preacher and Pentecostal ran for the Republican presidential nomination in 1988.

The new rise of the **Christian Right** began in the late 1960s and 1970s – when conservative Christians saw American principles undermined by permissiveness and decadence. To campaign for a revival of basic moral values Jerry Falwell called his group Moral Majority. The conservative and often fundamentalist TV evangelists demand a literal belief in the words of the Bible, believing that Jesus Christ will once again reign on earth. In their moral crusades they speak out against abortion, gay rights, pornography, and immoral behaviour in general. As the TV evangelists have acquired the status of stars and try to influence people's attitudes and voting behaviour, it is not surprising that their steps are closely watched by opposing and less conservative circles. More than once the Sunday priests became subjects of national controversy when scandals in which they were involved were made public. The press questioned their moral integrity and exposed them as hypocrites. In 1988 evangelist Jim Bakker was disgraced and had to give up his popular TV show. Falwell was heavily criticized because he had exaggerated his educational background and had falsified the date of his marriage to conceal the fact that his first child had been conceived out of wedlock. Swaggart was caught up in a scandal and considered stepping down from his ministry in 1991, but later announced that the Lord had told him to continue. Be it as it may, religious radio and television broadcasting have become a major feature of contemporary American religion and an important component of American society.

Religious Lobbying

The high political significance of the Electronic Church lies in the fact that it strengthens the religious right in the United States. Its most fervent supporters are to be found in the so-called "**Bible Belt**" in the South of the US. In early 2000, conservative religious groups put pressure on TV stations to ban the screening of a cartoon series in which God was portrayed as an amiable character, wearing dark sun glasses and a green T-shirt. Protesters in the deeply religious areas in the southern states attacked the animation show as "tasteless and trivial". TV stations in Utah, Idaho, Missouri, Indiana and Louisiana were the first to cancel the programme. In 1925 a biology teacher was taken to court for teaching the theory of evolution at a public school. Although the Court ruled in favour of the teacher a number of American states including Nebraska, Alabama, Kentucky, Oklahoma and Kansas have in recent years altered their educational policies regarding the teaching of Charles Darwin's theory. In his famous book *On the Origin of Species by Means of Natural Selection* (1859) Darwin argued that all forms of life on Earth developed from common ancestors. Over billions of years, life gradually evolved into the incredible variety of forms and species that exist today, including human beings. Fundamentalist Christian groups reject this theory as anti-religious because it conflicts with the biblical story that God created the world and all forms of life over a period of seven days. These views are known as creationism. State committees that review textbooks for use in public schools demanded that students should also be informed extensively on alternative views of the origins of life. There is little doubt in the scientific community today that Darwin's evolutionary theory is correct. The debate, however, shows that certain religious groups exert a great influence on public opinion and consequently on politics.

Some people observe the activities of the radical religious groups with suspicion and are worried about their increasing influence. In the 1980s groups of the Christian Right began drumming up support for conservative candidates in elections. Because he promised to support the establishment of school prayer and anti-abortion legislation Republican hardliner Ronald Reagan secured the support of conservative voters in the Bible Belt to achieve electoral victories in the 1980 and 1984 presidential elections. Although members of the Religious Right lobbied politicians massively and tried to put pressure on them to make laws and legislation less liberal, in reality their efforts had little effect. Once elected, US politicians have hardly ever given in to religious lobbying. When Bill Clinton, a Southern Baptist and an active member of Immanuel Baptist Church, Little Rock, Arkansas, ran for the presidency in 1992 he made it clear that he was a firm believer and often used religious metaphors in his public speeches. The hopes, which the Religious Right had put in him were disappointed, because Clinton introduced liberal legislation regarding homosexuality and abortion. From then on many conservative evangelicals and fundamentalists viewed him with suspicion and deep-seated antipathy. In 1998 when Clinton vetoed a bill which was intended to ban late–term abortion, he was heavily criticized by leaders of several religious groups including his own denomination, the **Southern Baptist Convention**. However, Clinton stood by his decision and was even supported by 36 religious leaders in the **Religious Coalition for Reproductive Choice**. It seems that the new leaders of today's Religious Right, such as Ralph Reed of Christian Coalition, have given up the direct lobbying methods of the 1980s. They have learned from the failures of their spiritual predecessors and today apply shrewder and more sensitive measures.

These examples show that the American people watch developments in the field of religion with open eyes. The vivid discussions and controversies are ample proof that the Constitutional separation of church and state which was laid down in the First Amendment has made religion stronger and not weaker. Religion is a more vigorous institution in the United States than in almost any other country where state and church are closely linked.

Media

The Press

The Freedom of the Press

A love-struck woman jumps out of a high window rather than face the bullying crowd of hard-faced journalists, the "rat-pack". Reporters beg a sheriff to bring forward an execution so they can write their reports in time for the morning papers. These are incidents in the play *The Front Page* written by Ben Hecht and Charles MacArthur, who worked as journalists in Chicago. The play is set in the 1920s and is a bitter satire on the lack of ethics of the tabloid press. The play was recently revived in many theatres in Britain and in the US following the doubtful and sad role parts of the press played in the O. J. Simpson trial or the prying into the private life of Diana, Princess of Wales. The 1920s and 1930s were a time of stiff competition between American newspapers, and the type of journalism exposed in the play *The Front Page* is called "**yellow journalism**". The term is used to describe the use of shocking features and sensationalized news in newspaper publishing to attract readers and increase circulation. Newspapers and magazines which concentrate on gossip are often referred to as the "**yellow press**" ('Regenbogenpresse'). However, not all papers employ ruthless methods in their pursuit of a sensational headline, serious journalism is an important cornerstone in any democracy. It is no wonder that in a dictatorship the media are kept under strict control and the freedom of the press is suppressed. Thomas Jefferson, one of the Founding Fathers of the United States, even went so far as to write: "If it were left to me to decide whether we should have a government without a free press or a free press without a government, I would prefer the latter." Jefferson and his political friends believed that it was the fundamental right of citizens to be informed about all sides of an issue without governmental interference. This conviction of the importance of the freedom of the press is laid down in the First Amendment to the Constitution of the United States: "Congress shall make no law respecting an establishment of religion, or prohibiting the free exercise thereof; or abridging the freedom of speech, or of the press; or the right of the people peaceably to assemble, and to petition the government for a redress of grievances". These words are the basis for America's tradition of a free press.

History of the Press in the USA

The founders of the United States thought it essential to stress the importance of an uncensored press in order to distinguish their new government from that of England. They remembered only too well what had happened to the first newspaper published in the American colonies. The paper *Publick Occurrences Both Forreign and Domestick* was launched in 1690 in Boston, Massachusetts, but was forced to close down by the colonial government after just one issue. It took fourteen years before John Campbell was allowed to print the first regularly published colonial newspaper, *The Boston News-Letter*. The British continued to censor the press and prosecuted persons who dared to criticize the British Crown. To comply with the strict regulations, American editors avoided controversy and restricted the contents of their papers to local news (birth, deaths) and social events. With the passing of the **Stamp Act of 1765** the British levied a direct tax on all papers required for official business in the American colonies. This tax was also put on newspapers in order to make them more expensive and thus reduce their circulation. The Stamp Act provoked riots and although it was repealed in 1766 it increased the resistance of the colonists against their English masters – a resistance which eventually culminated in the **American War of Independence**. In 1776 the editors of the colonial papers printed the **Declaration of Independence** on the front pages to demonstrate their support of the revolutionary movement. In the 19th century millions of immigrants arrived in the United States and the number of people who wanted to read a newspaper to learn about the American way of life increased rapidly. As new printing presses were invented and the railways made rapid transport across the country possible, more papers and cheaper papers could be printed and distributed. Newspaper publishing and advertising became a profitable business, and the number of American newspaper titles more than doubled between 1880 and 1900, from 850 to nearly 2,000.

One of the most difficult problems for many newly founded newspapers in the 19th century was how to gather news. This problem led to the founding of news services or 'wire services', whose business was to provide news and information for their subscribers. One of the largest and most successful was founded in London in 1851 by Paul Julius **Reuter**, who in 1858 began his service of foreign telegrams to the press. In the United States six New York newspapers formed the first news agency to be run by the newspapers themselves, the New York Associated Press in 1848, which after major changes became the **Associated Press** (**AP**). Today AP employs about 3,500 people working in 240 bureaus around the world and supplies a steady stream of news (20 million words a day) to its domestic members and foreign subscribers. Another American news service, **United Press International** (**UPI**), was created in 1958 by the merger of the **United Press Associations** (founded in 1907) and the **International News Service** (1909).

The rivalry between newspaper publishers Hearst and Pulitzer gave rise to a type of sensational journalism, called yellow journalism.

All immigrants from Europe emigrating to America over a hundred years ago arrived at Ellis Island, and the first city they saw and lived in was New York. Millions travelled on from here, but people from different races (Italians, Germans, Argentineans) and different religions (Christians, Jews, Buddhists) stayed and made New York the most bustling place in the New World. Because of its extraordinary mixture New York has always held a singular position among America's cities and it became the birthplace for several of the newspapers which formed the character of modern American journalism. In 1835 the *New York Herald* was founded by James Gordon Bennett, who saw to it that his paper presented an exciting combination of news and views. There were plenty of residents wanting to read a paper in New York, so Horace Greeley began to publish *New York Tribune* in 1841. Towards the end of the 19th century Joseph Pulitzer and William Randolph Hearst arrived in New York and created a new type of newspaper with a broad appeal for the less educated industrial workers in New York's booming industries. To cater for the taste of a mass readership the popular papers carried more sensational news and entertaining sections. From 1895 on Hearst's *Morning Journal* and Pulitzer's *World* competed strongly against each other for the supremacy on the New York press market. Their fierce competition eventually resulted in the tactics of yellow journalism, a phrase which derives from a comic strip named "The Yellow Kid", which played a part in the rivalry.

Joseph Pulitzer (1847–1911) was one of the most powerful newspaper editors and publishers in the United States and helped establish the pattern of the modern newspaper. He arrived in the US in 1864 from Hungary, fought in the American Civil War (1861–1865), studied law and turned to journalism. In 1883 he bought the failing *New York World* and increased its circulation by making the paper both informative (reports about political corruption) and entertaining (comics, sports coverage, women's fashion coverage, and illustrations). In his will Pulitzer provided for establishing the Columbia **School of Journalism** and the **Pulitzer Prize**, which has been awarded annually since 1917 for outstanding public service and achievement in American journalism, letters, and music. Pulitzer's opponent was William Randolph Hearst (1863–1951) with his *New York Morning Journal*. Hearst was born in San Francisco where in 1887 he started his career as newspaper editor by taking over his father's ailing paper *San Francisco Examiner*. With his sensationalist style he soon earned enough money to buy the *New York Morning Journal*. Hearst started a number of other profitable papers and magazines (*Cosmopolitan, Good Housekeeping, Town and Country*, and *Harper's Bazaar*) which grew into an empire comprising 20 major newspapers, telegraphic news facilities (the **International News Service** was started in 1909), radio stations, and news and motion picture syndicates. In 1941 Orson Welles used the life of media magnate Hearst as the model for Charles Foster Kane, the main character in his film *Citizen Kane*. Hearst unsuccessfully tried to suppress the film which is generally considered one of the greatest American movies ever made. **Hearst Newspapers** is one of the biggest newspaper chains in the US today.

In 1923 Henry Luce and Briton Hadden started their weekly news magazine *Time* which reported on political events, cultural activities, sports, movies, personalities, and specific social issues. The success of *Time* prompted other companies to start similar magazines. *Newsweek* was founded in 1933. Both are still the best known news magazines in the US, and they became the models of the German equivalent *Der Spiegel*, which began publication in 1947. Henry Luce was also the founder of another news magazine which he called *Life*, in 1936. *Life* was different in as much as its emphasis was on pictures, not the written word. The German journalist Henri Nannen created *Stern* in 1948 using *Life* as model.

The British are keen newspaper readers, and a number of British dailies have a circulation of several million copies. Things are different in the United States. The largest newspapers (*The Wall Street Journal* and *US Today*) sell about 1.7 million copies each. The reason for these relatively small circulation figures is that Americans mostly get their information about current events from watching television. Consequently, since the arrival of this medium in the late 1950s and early 1960s readership of newspapers has steadily declined. Many publishers ran into economic difficulties and eventually ceased publication of their papers. In 1960 eight major dailies were published in New York – by 1980 there were only four left. The same happened in other cities. Chicago once had four dailies, today there are two. Many newspapers saw their only chance of survival in printing regional and local news which would not be covered by the TV news programmes and news channels. This is why

American readers can choose from a large number of regional papers, but the US national press does not offer the same variety as the British. The pressure of rising production costs, including higher wages for the workers, and poor management drove many dailies out of business. Many editors and publishers saw the only way to survive in combining forces with others. This marked the beginning of the big newspaper chains, of which there are about 170 today. By 1980 60 per cent of the daily newspapers in the United States were owned by chains, today the figure has risen to more than 75 per cent. The largest newspaper chain is the **Gannett Company**, whose flagship newspaper, *USA Today*, is the largest-selling daily newspaper in the country. The Gannett Company owns some 90 newspapers with an overall circulation of more than 7 million worldwide. Other chains include Hearst Newspapers, Knight-Ridder Newspapers, the New York Times Company, the Times-Mirror Company, Thomson Newspapers, and Walls Newspapers.

In the 50s and 60s it was television which presented a threat to the existence of newspapers, today it is the rapid and widespread expansion of the Internet. Most papers have online versions which can be read on the Internet free of charge. This is possible because the Internet pages carry advertisements, which help to finance the enterprise. Free email newsletters and other online services have further contributed to the decline in newspaper subscriptions and circulation rates. It is estimated that the percentage of Americans getting news from the Internet at least once a week more than tripled between 1996 and 1998 – from 11 million readers to 36 million readers. Although some media experts predict that within the next decades printed newspaper will be replaced entirely by electronic information services, others maintain that the printed word will never disappear and remain an important part of our modern information society.

Most innovations in the field of communication software originate from firms which have their main offices and think tanks in an area in north-western California between Palo Alto and San José, called **Silicon Valley**. The name is used because the chemical silicon is widely used in the production of electronic devices. Since the 1990s Silicon Valley has been the world centre for electronics, computing, and database systems, although its computer-related history dates back as far as 1939, when Stanford University engineers Bill Hewlett and David Packard started producing electronic equipment. The enormous success of the high-tech firms in Silicon Valley is illustrated by the fact that many new jobs are being created and the export rate is booming. In the meantime other industries have settled in Silicon Valley as well, e. g. biotechnology and environmental science.

The Role of a Free Press

The press is regarded as the fourth authority in a democratic state – the other three are the legislative, executive and judicial powers. It informs the public on important events and, to a certain extent, exercises control on the government and local administration. In recent years parts of the press have appointed themselves the role of watchdogs over morals and decent behaviour. The personal conduct of film stars, sportsmen, TV personalities or politicians is scrutinised and every faltering step or offence against decency is ruthlessly exposed. TV evangelists had to retire from their shows because of immoral conduct. President Clinton's affair with a young White House trainee made the headlines in 1998, and was so widely publicised that legal procedures were taken to remove the president from office on **impeachment**. Very often it is not so much a fight for honesty and good manners, which makes the press pry into people's lives, but the need to increase circulation or ratings by satisfying the public's hunger for sensation. Dragging people's personal failures into the limelight is a sign of bad taste and a false interpretation of the role of the press. Two recent examples from US history stand out as triumphs of investigative journalism and illustrate the vital role a free press plays in the control of the government.

The uncovering of the Watergate scandal which eventually led to the first resignation of a US President – Richard M. Nixon – is one of the triumphs of serious 'investigative' journalism.

Reporters and journalists of two of the most respected papers in the United States, *The Washington Post* and the *New York Times*, informed the public about events which the governments of the day would have liked to conceal. The two spectacular investigations and publications of the journalists became known worldwide as the **Watergate Scandal** and the **Pentagon Papers Affair**. In 1971, the *New York Times* obtained a copy of a top-secret document which outlined the history of America's war in Vietnam. The classified document, called the Pentagon Papers, had been prepared by the Department of Defence. On June 13, 1971, the *New York Times* published excerpts from the secret study, which suggested that the government had misled the American people about the war. The day after the series began, the editor of the paper received a telegram from the US attorney general who claimed that the publication of the information violated the **Espionage Law** and caused "irreparable injury to the defence interests of the United States". The government took the paper to court. In the case *New York Times* Co. versus United States the Supreme Court ruled that the publication of the papers could continue and thus upheld the right of the press to perform its function as a check on official power.

During the presidential campaign of 1972 five burglars led by a former **CIA** (**Central Intelligence Agency**) employee broke into a hotel and office complex, the Watergate, in Washington, where the **Democratic Party** had its headquarters. They were working for the **Republican Party's Committee to Re-Elect the President**, then Richard M. Nixon (in office 1968–1974). With extraordinary persistence and accuracy two *Washington Post* reporters, Carl Bernstein and Bob Woodward, traced the connections of the burglars to the White House. They revealed that high officials who were very close to President Nixon were involved in the planning and the execution of the burglary. At first Nixon and his aides denied any involvement in the Watergate break-in, but with their investigations the reporters finally proved that President Nixon himself was aware of illegal measures to cover up the affair. When Nixon realised that he was likely to be impeached and removed, he resigned. For their coverage of the political scandal that led to the first resignation of a president in US history, Bernstein and Woodward won for the *Washington Post* the 1973 Pulitzer Prize for public service. Together they wrote the bestseller, *All the President's Men* (1974), which was made into a successful film, starring Robert Redford and Dustin Hoffman.

Television

In Britain thousands of people bought their first TV sets in 1953 to watch the coronation of Queen Elizabeth II on the screen at home. In the US the broadcast of baseball's **World Series** in 1947 started the new age of television as a mass media. Today the most important networks are the **National Broadcasting Company** (**NBC**) – which dominates the ratings –, the **Columbia**

Broadcasting System (CBS), the **American Broadcasting Company** (ABC) – owned by the Disney company –, the **Fox Broadcasting Company**. The 24-hour news station **Cable News Network** (CNN) was launched on cable television in 1980 by Ted Turner. Apart from these channels there are rising numbers of cable networks and programmers whose shows can be received via satellite. All stations are commercial stations financed entirely by advertising revenue, which means the TV companies sell time for advertisements which are broadcast in breaks during programmes. The phrases with which the commercials are introduced usually are: "We'll be back after a short break ..." or "Now a short message from our sponsor ...". The only non-commercial station is the **Public Broadcasting System (PBS)**. TV advertising is expensive and firms spend enormous sums to advertise during a special event such as the **Super Bowl** because the programme is watched by millions of viewers. As soon as a programme or a show loses its popularity it is taken off the air. Special organizations (e. g. Nielsen Media Research) establish the ratings of the programmes and inform TV producers and advertisers. In order to attract as many viewers as possible TV programming is concentrated on entertainment and diversion. Popular shows include family situation comedies (sitcoms such as the classic *I Love Lucy*, *The Cosby Show*, *Seinfeld, Ally McBeal* and *Friends*) and comedy-variety shows featuring well-known performers. There are all sorts of adventure series for example Westerns (*Bonanza*, the longest running was *Gunsmoke*, which lasted from 1955 until 1975), detective series such as *Columbo*, *Kojak*, *Miami Vice* and *NYPD Blue*, science fiction series such as *Star Trek*, which was started in 1963, and hospital shows which include *Marcus Welby, M.D.* and *E.R.*

A more recent development are the so-called soap operas, which were first produced for radio and daytime television. The name derives from the fact that the first sponsors of such shows were soap manufacturers. In 1978 CBS screened the first weekly soap at prime-time (after 8 o'clock at night), *Dallas.* Its success led to the creation of many similar shows (*Dynasty*). Quiz and game shows enjoy a consistent popularity, as do talk shows. Famous talk show hosts are Johnny Carson and David Letterman, whose late-night show is the model of Harald Schmidt's German version. Today Larry King, alias Lawrence Harvey Zeiger (born 1933 in Brooklyn to Russian-Jewish emigré parents), is probably the most renowned interviewer in the world. His show *Larry King Live* can be watched on CNN in 170 million households in 210 countries around the world. Over the years he has interviewed almost all of the prominent people in the world – from Mikhail Gorbachev to Frank Sinatra and Yasser Arafat, from the Dalai Lama to the Duchess of York and Gerry Adams, from Clinton to Thatcher. Although heavily criticized because its participants do less talking and more fighting *The Jerry Springer Show* has become one of today's top-rated talk shows, surpassing long-time talk queen *Oprah Winfrey*. The coverage of sporting events always attracts the greatest number of viewers. Most major sports, wrestling and the latest movies and hit series can be watched – and must be paid for by taking out a subscription – on cable channels such as USA Network. The extraordinary rise of cable networks and the increase in the number of people who have subscribed to cable (in 1998 about 70 per cent of all US homes with TV) is the greatest challenge to the big three TV companies NBC, CBS, ABC, all of which continue to lose viewers.

Television and Elections

Most Americans today rely on cable and television news programmes as their primary sources of information. Six out of ten say that television is their main source of information about elections, government, and current events; newspapers are less important – only one US citizen out of ten keeps up with current affairs predominately through newspapers. Television attracts an enormous audience that no other mode of communication in the United States can match. The average American watches three hours of television daily and there is a television set in almost all households. The fact that this medium reaches into 220 million households makes television the most important medium for politicians and also the most cost-effective way of communicating with the electorate. During campaigns for the US Senate or presidential elections extensive advertising crusades are launched to win the support of the independent and still undecided voters. In the extremely close race for the presidency in 2000 the two contestants, Texas Governor George W. Bush and Vice President Al Gore, faced each other in four TV debates. Hundreds of analysts and consultants worked in the election committees of the two rivals to prepare them for the TV appearances. Media experts say, the visual impact of the electronic medium is so great that viewers pay more attention to how the speakers look, what facial expressions and gestures they make than to what they actually say. To describe this fact Marshall McLuhan (1911–1980) coined the phrase "the medium is the message". In 1960 the first presidential TV debate was held and decided the presidential race between John F. Kennedy and Richard Nixon. Nixon had charged his opponent that he was too young and too inexperienced to serve as president. However, in the disputes Kennedy made a much better impression on the audience and the debates turned the tables. Kennedy won the elections in November 1960 and became the nation's first real "television president" who used the new medium for his political aims. For the first time he allowed live broadcasts of news conference to convey his policies of the "New Frontier" to the American people. Since then clever strategies have been developed to make politics understandable and attractive for the average viewer. In particular at election times, politics is "made for television", which means it is simplified and reduced for the evening news. Long debates and detailed discussions have disappeared. Many foreign observers fear that elections in their home countries will become like those in the United States. European party and election campaign managers are already hiring the know-how of the men and women who manage presidential campaigns in the US. Tony Blair first used these "spin doctors" in the 1997 General Election in the United Kingdom. In 1998 Germany's Social Democrats introduced American-style show elements (music, lighting, colours) into their campaign which eventually helped Gerhard Schröder to be elected Bundeskanzler.

Economy – Agriculture and Industry

Today the United States has the world's most powerful and technologically advanced economy, the efficiency and productivity of which exceeds that of all other countries. The commonest way for economists to measure the economic strength and also the degree of development of a country is by reference to its **Gross National Product** (**GNP**). The GNP is the volume of goods (such as automobiles, TV sets, washing machines) and services (such as education, medical services, hotel accommodation, air travel, etc.) produced by the work force of a country in a year. In order to be able to compare and rank larger and smaller countries, the GNP is expressed per head of population. Towards the end of the 1990s the GNP per head in the USA was about $31,500, in Germany it amounted to $22,100, and in the United Kingdom to $21,200. At the bottom of the table are the poorest countries in the world such as Pakistan with $2,000 and Bangladesh with $1,380 GNP per capita. As a result of the strength of their economy Americans enjoy the highest standard of living in the world – generally speaking. US firms are at the forefront in technological advances, they are world leaders in computer and aerospace technology, in the development and production of medical and military equipment.

Until the colonial era European countries, above all Great Britain, were the world leaders in economy. That leadership was lost to the United States for several reasons. First of all, the American government did not interfere with people's economic activities, there were hardly any business regulations or limitations. What is more, the country had **generous tax laws** which made it easy and profitable for private individuals or investors to set up firms and businesses in the New World. The **liberal regulations** and the prospect of relatively quick success attracted millions of immigrants. America was the land of open opportunities, free from class barriers and privileges based on heredity, so that people could concentrate on business. President Calvin Coolidge said in 1925: "The business of America is business". Another factor which explains the rise of the US economy is the fact that American firms profited from an ever-growing **consumer market**. Due to the immigration waves during the 19th century the American population increased tremendously and consequently the number of prospective customers. Today US firms can sell their products and services to more than 250 million consumers who live right at their doorstep. In contrast, economies in the Old World lost much of their power in the post-colonial era mainly as a result of their comparatively small size. It took until the end of the 20th century before the European countries managed to counterbalance this enormous advantage of US companies by creating a monetary union and a single market within the European Community.

Agriculture

Agricultural Belts

The natural environmental conditions which are necessary for farming – such as soil, climate, and topography – determine the crops produced, the techniques employed, and the type of farm organization. The especially advantaged areas for farming in the United States are the so-called agricultural belts, vast stretches of land which follow climatic zones. The **Dairy Belt** extends through the green pastures of New England and the Great Lakes area and provides milk products (cheese and butter) for the big cities of New York and Chicago. The climate in the Dairy Belt area is rather moist, the growing season is short and the thin glacial soil less suited to arable farming. The **Corn (Maize) Belt**, sometimes referred to as the bread basket of the world, runs through the Midwestern United States from the Allegheny Mountains to Missouri and occupies the country's largest continuous body of fertile level land. Farming in this region produces cheap, good-quality maize, beef and many other sorts of farm produce. The **Wheat Belt** in the Great Plains west of the Mississippi is one of the world's chief granaries. More than once, US farmers helped nations confronted with a hunger crisis to overcome their problems by supplying them with wheat grown in abundance in the Wheat Belt. Spring wheat grows west of Lake Superior and the Prairie Provinces of Canada, winter wheat is produced from northern Texas to Missouri. The **Cotton Belt** extends through the south of the eastern USA from North Carolina to Texas. Because of inefficient farming methods and monoculture the soil in the Cotton Belt was often exhausted in the past. As a consequence, many farmers and farm workers had to leave their land and migrate to the industrial North to find work in the factories there. Today, more up-to-date farming methods are applied. **Fertilization** and **rotation** with other crops like peanuts have helped to revitalize the soil.

Because of its vast wheat fields Kansas has been called the Wheat State and the Breadbasket of America. Huge machines are used to bring in the harvest.

The Ups and Downs of US Agriculture

The basis of the formidable success of the US economy was laid in a sector which has changed dramatically over the last 200 years: in agriculture. At the time of the **War of Independence** (1775–1783) the Americans were a nation of farmers: 95 per cent of the population was engaged in agriculture. Peasants and smallholders left their European homelands in great numbers because most of the land was in the hands of the landed gentry. The prospect of changing from tenant to land owner made millions leave for the New World where conditions for agriculture were ideal in most parts of the country. Land was abundant, but there were not enough people to work on it, so farms, which were mainly run by the farmer and his family, were scattered over enormous areas of land. These isolated family farms became the basis of North American agriculture, and their owners developed a strong sense of individualism and self-reliance.

Throughout the 19th century new tools and equipment were invented and new techniques introduced. Machines were taking over the work of haying, threshing, mowing, cultivating, and planting. Cyrus McCormick's mechanical reaper ('Erntemaschine') changed the production methods on American farms. Apart from making life easier for the farmers these new inventions also helped to boost the agricultural output considerably. Productivity was further pushed by the arrival of more settlers. The **Homestead Act** of 1862 promoted westward migration across the Mississippi River by maintaining the existing pattern of small family farms by offering a "homestead" of 65 hectares to each family of settlers for a nominal fee. In the end the government had achieved more than it had intended, because farms produced more than that which was needed and after the Civil War overproduction became a serious problem. As a result prices fell and farmers received less for their products. However, things improved, in particular because the federal government created the Department of Agriculture in 1862 which took a direct role in agricultural affairs.

In the 1920s and 1930s American farmers again experienced desperate decades. The average income per head in the USA in 1929 was $681; the average farmer's income was $273, because farmers had become the victims of their own success. During the years of the **First World War** farmers had increased production to sell food to Europe. They had cultivated new land, taken on new machinery. When the war was over Europe was growing its food again and US farmers were producing more than they could sell. As a consequence prices for agricultural products fell dramatically. It was not worth taking crops to the market, because freight costs were higher than the prices farmers could

Franklin Delano Roosevelt was the only President elected four times. When he was 39, Roosevelt was stricken with infantile paralysis (polio). Although he recovered partial use of his legs, he could never stand again without help.

achieve for their produce. Tens of thousands of farmers could not meet their mortgage repayments and were driven into bankruptcy. In his novel *The Grapes of Wrath* (1939; Pulitzer Prize, 1940) the American writer John Steinbeck tells the dramatic and emotionally gripping story of a family from the impoverished Oklahoma Dust Bowl during the economic depression of the 1930s. The Joads are a family of sharecroppers who leave their eroded, dust-bowl farm in Oklahoma and come to the promised land of California, where they become the lowest of the migratory farm labourers. With his **New Deal Action Programme** of 1933 President Franklin Delano Roosevelt saved many farmers and their families. After his election to the presidency in 1932 he promised to restore the confidence of the American people and to bring America out of the **Great Depression**. Roosevelt stated in his first inaugural address that "we have nothing to fear but fear itself". In a number of radio talks, the so-called "fireside chats", he addressed the American people, explaining the legislation of his administration. In his second chat he presented a plan to relieve the plight of the American farmers.

A newly created government agency, the **Agricultural Adjustment Administration** (AAA), set fixed quotas for most agricultural products to avoid overproduction and thus keep the price of farm produce up. Pigs were slaughtered, the cotton crop was ploughed into the ground, and farmers were paid not to cultivate some land. Parts of Roosevelt's rescue plans have been incorporated into today's farm policies of the federal government in Washington that promotes up-to-date farming techniques. The Depression of the thirties has also made farmers change from monoculture to a greater diversity in farming, because it makes them less vulnerable to climatic hazards and crises in the world market.

From Family Farms to Agribusiness

The small immigrant farmer who used to work on his land to provide for himself and his family has disappeared almost completely. Today large corporations own the land and use modern machinery to improve the agricultural output. Manual labour has been reduced, draught animals have been replaced by machines. Farming has been lifted from the self-survival level to a commercial level. It has become big business and therefore been given a new name: people speak of **agribusiness**. The agribusiness sector is much larger than the traditional farming industry. It is not only concerned with the production, purchasing and marketing of foods, it also fabricates and sells fertilizers, insecticides and supplies machinery and equipment. The development of improved techniques in the areas of irrigation, soil analysis, fertilisation, plant and animal breeding and the application of advanced managerial methods have raised agricultural production to such a high level that a single farmer can grow enough food to feed himself, 45 other Americans and 8 foreigners. Today less than 3 per cent of the population work on farms in the United States, but produce more than can be consumed in the country. One-third of the cropland in the United States produces crops destined for export. In 1995 agricultural exports exceeded imports by nearly two to one.

Chemical Farming

The production methods in US agriculture have exacted their price. Above all, conservationists criticize that American farmers have damaged the environment because they use large amounts of artificial fertilizers and chemicals to kill weeds and pests. In colonial days, the farmer pushed his seed corn into the ground with a stick and fertilized it with a fish. The modern farmer of today has been taught by agricultural experts that the best way to increase output is to use **chemical fertilizer** and then protect the harvest from insects with generous applications of pesticides. It is not surprising then that toxic chemicals used in agriculture have found their way into the nation's water, food and air. Even more worrying is the fact that the giant poultry, hog and cattle factories are not merely producing meat, they are also producing a horrendous crop of drug-resistant germs. The problem is the overdosing of farm animals with antibiotics to kill bacteria in the animals. About half of the antibiotics produced in the United States are being used in animals – and 80 per cent of these are used not to fight animal diseases, but merely to stimulate quick growth. Scientists are concerned that the strongest germs might mutate and become completely resistant to antibiotics. Recent studies of the US Agriculture Department have found that farmers who apply few or no chemicals to crops are usually as productive as those who use pesticides and synthetic fertilizers.

Genetically Modified (GM) Crops

At present, scientists at biotechnology research centres across the United States are working on innovative techniques which can be applied in agriculture. They are developing so-called "**genetically modified (GM) crops**" by inserting genetic material from one species of plant, bacteria, virus, animal or fish into another species. Scientists hope that GM crops will help to fight hunger and poverty particularly in developing countries. To this end the **US Agency for International Development** spends $ 7 million yearly on agricultural biotechnology in Third World countries. Genetically modified (GM) crops will grow more rapidly and eventually increase yields. As these new plants will also be resistant to pests farmers will have to use less toxic chemicals, so that they can produce healthier food. Agricultural experts are convinced that by using GM crops the levels of nutrition can be improved, because our food will contain more vitamins, and it can thus help prevent disease.

Although it is commonly agreed that biotechnology can increase food production and fight disease, there are still many unsolved questions. One of the most outspoken critics of over-intensified agriculture and an advocate of organic farming in Great Britain is the Prince of Wales. Modifying genes, he argues, is taking mankind into realms that belong to God alone. He believes that agriculture should proceed in harmony with nature, because we simply do not know the long-term consequences for human health and the wider environment when we release modified plants into nature. Critics warn we might cause 'genetic pollution', because genetically engineered crop plants are capable of transferring their genetic qualities to wild plants. This transfer might eventually create 'super-weeds' which could disrupt the **natural biodiversity** of an area. People's reservations are also based on the fact that we do not yet have adequate laws and regulations for the application of biotechnology in foods. In view of the public's worries the US Administration improved safety standards for meat, poultry, seafood products, for fruit and vegetable juices to ensure that Americans eat the safest possible food.

In spite of the improved legislation critics maintain that by using genetically modified crops we run incalculable risks because the health effects of eating genetically engineered foodstuffs are, as yet, unknown. The BSE scandal in Britain and other man-made disasters in the cause of 'cheap food' should have taught people the lesson that man's interference with nature can have disastrous effects. Once the damage has been done, it is not only difficult and expensive to restore people's health and well-being – sometimes it is even impossible. When in early 2000 a relatively high number of young people from one region in mid-England showed symptoms of Creuzfeldt-Jakob-Disease and a few eventually died of the fatal illness it was suspected that baby food and school dinners they had eaten in the Eighties had contained contaminated meat.

Industry

19th century: Industrial Expansion and Economic Rise

The **Industrial Revolution** occurred in Britain between 1750 and 1850. It was a revolution which changed production methods and also transformed the country from a rural to an urban civilisation. **Industrialisation** in the United States differed in several ways. It did not bring about a radical change of society, as there was no European-style society, characterised by the gap between aristocratic rich and labouring poor, to change. American industrialisation was not based on the invention of new tools and machines: Americans adopted and improved innovations already used in Europe. Finally, the growth of American industry happened at the same time as the growth of the American nation and could therefore be better planned. The waves of immigration increased the country's population and provided a steady stream of workers who contributed to the expansion of business and industry. However, the population growth was not so fast as to overwhelm the economy. Therefore workers' slums, as in British cities, did not develop in the USA.

In colonial times the British used their North American colonies as suppliers of raw materials. American businesses were forbidden to manufacture, because the British had reserved the right to finish the goods in their factories at home. From here they could sell the manufactured products at much higher prices than they had paid for the raw materials. Farming and trading were therefore the main businesses in the United States until the mid-1800s when in the course of the Napoleonic Wars (1803–1815) British goods were hard to obtain and the United States had to produce most of its own goods, with the textile industry in New England becoming the first important industrial sector. The **Civil War** and the **building of the railroads** further spurred industrialisation in the United States. It is undeniable, the war between the **Yankees** and the **Confederates** claimed the lives of tens of thousands of people and devastated the economy in the South,

The building of a system of railroad lines between 1870 and 1900 facilitated the conquest of the West.

but it nevertheless stimulated industrial development, mainly in the North-east. Uniforms, shoes and, above all, weapons were needed to outfit the large number of soldiers. It was Eli Whitney who developed a new method to produce firearms by designing a gun of identical parts and machinery which allowed unskilled workers to put the parts together. Whitney revolutionised manufacturing and American manufacturers soon adopted his system in other sectors of industry, thus making mass production possible. The second great stimulus came from the construction of the railroads which began in the 1830s. The pace of building accelerated after 1862, when Congress set aside public land for the first transcontinental railroad, generating a great demand for coal, iron, and steel. Railroads became increasingly important to the expanding nation as goods and heavy loads such as coal, iron ore and minerals could be transported fast and efficiently. The railroads linked out-lying areas of the country into the world's first transcontinental market and pioneers could spread their settlements into hitherto unconquered territories. Industrialisation in the new world had progressed to such an extent that by 1890 the output of America's factories exceeded the output of its farms. On the international level, Britain had lost its place as leading industrial country to Germany and the United States – two countries which had started industrialisation later, but with newer and more advanced machinery. By 1913 more than one-third of the world's industrial production came from the United States.

20th century: The World's No. 1 Industrial Power

Whereas the economies of Germany and other European countries were badly damaged due to the devastations of two world wars the US economy profited from the war effort in Europe and managed to become the greatest productive country in the world. Until 1917 the US stayed out of the First World War and did well selling weapons, ammunition and food to the warring nations of Europe, the profits being invested in new industries. Using innovative production methods such as the assembly-line, manufacturers could produce consumer goods – cars, radios, vacuum cleaners – faster and more cheaply. Lower costs also meant lower prices for consumers and higher wages for the workers. Thus more and more Americans were able to afford products which for a long time had been regarded as luxury items, revolutionising the American way of life in the roaring twenties. The car, chemical and film industries experienced unprecedented booms which were supported by new techniques developed by the advertising industry (radio commercials, posters, commercial travellers) to persuade people to buy the new products.

However, large sections of society, in particular farmers, blacks and the unemployed, did not share in the country's prosperity. When eventually even more people lost their jobs and so did not have the money to buy consumer goods the US economy faced a serious crisis, the most spectacular sign of which was the Wall Street crash in October 1929. This collapse of the US stock market marked the beginning of the **Great Depression**. During his campaign for the presidency in 1932 F. D. Roosevelt promised a "**New Deal**" for the country to help "the forgotten man", the farmer who had lost his land or the worker who had lost his job. After his election Roosevelt introduced new laws to restore people's confidence in the banking system, to create jobs for the masses of unemployed and help the impoverished farmers. Although some laws were invalidated by the Supreme Court, Roosevelt set up the **Second New Deal** which finally helped the US economy to recover.

In the course of the 20th century industries in the United States performed differently. Some branches flourished, others faced serious challenges. The car industry and the textile industry for example had to fight competition from foreign countries, above all Japan, where labour costs were lower. On the other hand, new sectors developed and boomed. Manufacturers of airplanes, cellular telephones, microchips and space satellites, microwave ovens and high-speed computers netted high profits. One of the reasons for the success of the manufacturing industries was the high degree of automation, which meant fewer workers were needed than in traditional industries and production costs were cut, making the goods cheaper. Today a new sector is gaining more and more importance: the service industry, which includes banking, insurance and finance services, entertainment and recreation, hotels and restaurants, communications, education and office administration. Economists argue that selling a service will become more important than making a product and that America is changing into a "post-industrial" society.

The American Idea of Free Enterprise

Since the days of the Founding Fathers and the pioneers Americans have placed high value on the idea of individual liberty and self-reliance. This concept is also reflected in the American approach to economic matters: Everybody should be able to decide in which business to operate and be allowed to pursue profit freely – which above all meant without restraint from government intervention. The consequences of economic freedom and the function of market forces were explained by the economist and philosopher Adam Smith in his publication *An Inquiry into the Nature and Causes of the Wealth of Nations* (1776), the first major work of political economy. The economic doctrine advocating that commerce and trade should be permitted to operate free of controls of any kind was referred to as "laissez-faire" (which means 'leave alone to do') and became the corner stone of capitalism and has been the driving force behind the American economy. Americans still rely very much on private enterprise and initiative, although over the years more government regulation has been introduced into the economic system. A look at the lives and works of three American entrepreneurs serves as an illustration of the typically American economic spirit, which created the American Dream, the vision of the dishwasher who makes it to become a millionaire – a success story which many Americans believe is still possible today.

John Davison Rockefeller

J. D. Rockefeller (1839–1937) was the guiding force behind the creation and development of the **Standard Oil Company**, which grew to dominate the oil industry and became one of the first big trusts in the United States. He became a legend in his own lifetime and a rather controversial figure, because for some he remained the supreme American success story, for others he was the symbol of unrestrained capitalism. J. D. Rockefeller was born in Richford, N.Y. in 1839 as the second of six children of William A. and Eliza Rockefeller. The family lived in modest circumstances. School was difficult for the young Rockefeller and after only two years of high school he went to work in Cleveland, Ohio, in 1855 as a bookkeeper for a small food firm. In 1859 together with his partner Maurice B. Clark he formed Clark & Rockefeller, a food firm handling grain, hay, meat and other goods. Like many other businesses, their company prospered during the Civil War. As he was deeply religious, he began to give 10 per cent of his earnings to churches. In 1863 came "the day that determined my career", as he later said. Rockefeller gave up the meat and grain firm and entered the brand new oil business by setting up a refinery in Cleveland. In 1870 he founded the Standard Oil Company of Ohio, which soon grew into a complex organisation dominating almost every aspect of the oil business: the piping, refining, and marketing of American petroleum. In order to keep control of this industrial giant Rockefeller formed the first modern trust, the **Standard Oil Trust**, in 1882. The trust company was regarded as a monopoly whose monopolistic practices endangered free competition. Members of the public denounced Rockefeller as a dictator and ruthless businessman and the government eventually decided to take action. In 1890 Congress passed the **Sherman Act** – named after Senator John Sherman of Ohio –, the first of three antitrust laws. With this law the government wanted to ensure that market competition was not threatened by a organization or cartel with a monopoly on a given product. The other two major federal antitrust laws are the **Clayton Act** of 1914 and the **Federal Trade commission Act** of 1914. The federal lawsuit against Standard Oil ended in 1892 with the court's decision demanding the dissolution of the trust. Rockefeller dissolved the Standard Oil Trust and transferred control to companies in different states, but he maintained control through Standard Oil (New Jersey). In 1911 the Supreme Court forced the separation of the thirty-eight companies which Standard Oil controlled into individual firms. By this time Rockefeller had retired from active leadership in the company and become more engaged in his philanthropic activities. He gave away some $ 550 million of his fortune to the Baptist Church, the YMCA, the University of Chicago, and the Rockefeller Institute for Medical Research (since 1953 Rockefeller University).

Henry Ford

Henry Ford was the American industrialist who further developed Eli Whitney's technique for the production of firearms. He introduced the moving assembly line, thus setting up the factory system which is used throughout the United States and large parts of the world. Henry Ford was born on July 30, 1863, near Dearborn, Michigan, a few miles west of Detroit, the eldest of six children of William Ford, an Irishman who had fled to America when he was 21, and Mary Ford. Henry took an early interest in repairing machinery. At 17 he took a job in the Michigan Car Works and began building engines and motors in his spare time. Neighbours who heard him banging about in his workshop night after night called him 'Mad Henry'. In 1903, after a couple of false starts, he and his partners incorporated **Ford Motor Company** and started selling a few cars. His vision was, however, to build a car for the masses: an inexpensive, highly dependable, easy-to-repair car. Henry Ford used all his early profits to design his dream car, and in October 1908 presented his Model T, nicknamed "**Tin Lizzie**", which he offered for $ 825, about half the price of many other cars of the day. With Ford's Model T the era of mass production began. The increasing demand for the T made Ford devise the ideal way to manufacture it. He and his team introduced the modern assembly line, a method in which conveyor belts brought car parts to workers. When the system was first introduced the amount of time required to build a Model T could be reduced from 12 1/2 hours to 93 minutes, and later, by the mid-1920s, a T could be assembled in fewer than 30 seconds. The car's retail price dropped from $ 440 to $ 290. When the last Model T car left the factory in 1927, more than 15 million "Tin Lizzies" had been built. Henry Ford became one of the most famous men of his time, admired by millions and his **Ford**

Motor Company became the world's biggest car company. Industrial managers studied Ford's manufacturing techniques in order to break down work processes and design more efficient and less costly ways of organizing tasks. Ford's innovation was also criticized, because work on the assembly line can be monotonous and have a numbing effect on workers and bored, depressed workers tend to do inferior work. Charlie Chaplin satirized the new production method in his film *Modern Times* (1936). In today's car factories robots have taken over the boring routine jobs. Henry Ford did not only revolutionize production methods, he was also an innovator in labour policy. He introduced the minimum wage, the 8-hour-day and the 40-hour week. He died on April 7, 1947, at the age of 83.

By introducing the assembly line method of production Henry Ford could reduce the price for his Model T car from originally $825 to $290. As a result, more than half the cars sold in the United States in the 1920s were Fords.

Bill Gates

Americans don't like monopolies – and what happened more than one hundred years ago to Rockefeller's **Standard Oil** seems to have repeated itself in the US Department of Justice's action against computer software giant Microsoft. The company was founded by computer programmer William Henry Gates, whom many regard as the wealthiest man in America today. Bill Gates was born in Seattle in 1955 and wrote his first software programme when he was only 13. As a high school student he helped computerize the payroll system of his school. At age of 15 he founded Traf-O-Data, a company that constructed a device to control traffic patterns in Seattle which he sold to local governments. In 1975, when he was in his second year at Harvard University, Gates joined his hometown friend Paul G. Allen and began adapting **Basic**, a popular programming language used on large computers, for use on smaller personal computers (**PCs**). Later in the same year he dropped out of Harvard to devote his whole time writing programmes. In 1977, together with Allen, Gates founded **Microsoft** to develop and produce a computer operating system called **MS-DOS** (Microsoft Disk Operating System). The rise of the company began in 1981 when the world's biggest computer supplier **International Business Machines (IBM)** adopted Microsoft's software DOS for its line of personal computers. Gates was smart enough not to sell his software, but to license it to IBM, which means he was not paid in one lump sum, but he received revenues for every computer sold. Makers of IBM-compatible PCs, or clones, also turned to Microsoft for their basic software, so that by 1983 Gates had licensed DOS to more than 100 vendors, making it the dominant operating system. Before the age of 40 Gates had made tens of billions of dollars, which made him the world's richest private individual, but had little effect on his personal lifestyle. He owns a collection of expensive sports cars and built himself a $ 50 million computer-controlled private complex overlooking Lake Washington, but his main interests lie with computer programming and the potential of information technology. Gates takes an active role in the running of the business at Microsoft headquarters in Redmond, Washington. In 1995 he published his best-seller *The Road Ahead* where he observed, "Success is a lousy teacher. It seduces smart people into thinking they can't lose".

As Microsoft's products (Windows, Internet Explorer) began to dominate the market of computer operating programmes, many of Gates' rivals saw the influence and power of Microsoft with suspicion. Competing software firms (Netscape) accused Microsoft of restrictive trading practices aimed at maintaining a monopoly. This accusation attracted the attention of the antitrust division of the US Justice Department which started legal proceedings against Microsoft. The trial lasted 11 months and ended with the court's conclusion that the company was a monopoly and had behaved ruthlessly against competitors. These findings may lead to the breaking up of Microsoft into separate independent companies – then the company would share the same fate as John D. Rockefeller's Standard Oil Trust.

Labour and Management

Americans never developed the same class consciousness as workers in England, because for long time they believed in freedom and equality for all. This equality was also reflected in their workplace. In a small business shop or on a farm, workers and their bosses worked side by side. The industrialisation in the 19th century changed this relationship and led to the formation of **labor unions**. Many Americans first saw the unions with reservation, blaming them for violence and unrest, and the unions had to work hard to win public acceptance. This acceptance was gradually achieved, because life and working conditions for the industrial workers in America's factories became harder and harder. Only a fraction of the wealth which the growth of the nation generated went to its workers. As more machines were introduced into the production process (**assembly line**) the demand for skilled labour decreased, and unskilled workers were available in unprecedented numbers because millions of immigrants entered the country, ready to take any job available. In 1900, wages were low, hours long – most industrial workers worked a 10-hour day (12 hours in the steel industry) – , and working conditions hazardous. More factory workers suffered fatal accidents in the United States than in any industrialized nation in the world. Women and children who made up a high percentage of the work force in some industries were at a particular disadvantage because they often received but a small part of the wages a man could earn.

The first major effort to organize workers' groups on a nationwide basis appeared with **The Noble Order of the Knights of Labor** in 1869 whose place in the labour movement was gradually taken over by the **American Federation of Labor** (**AFL**). The AFL was founded in 1886 by Samuel Gompers, a leader of the Cigarmakers Union, and was only open to skilled workers. During the great industrial growth between 1865 and 1900, the work force expanded enormously, especially in the heavy industries and strikes, sometimes accompanied by violence, became commonplace. The first violent conflict between employers and workers occurred with the **Great Rail Strike** of 1877, when rail workers across the nation went out on strike in response to a 10 per cent pay cut. The most militant union was the **International Workers of the World** (**IWW**), which was founded in 1905 and whose members were commonly known as "Wobblies". The IWW openly called for class warfare and demanded the overthrow of capitalism through strikes, boycotts, and sabotage. A prominent member of the IWW was Joe Hill, who became a hero and legend of the labour movement. He was born in Sweden, migrated to the United States in 1902 and joined the IWW in 1910, five years after its formation. Over the next five years he campaigned for many working class causes and became a popular song-writer with a gift for capturing the meaning of these causes in song. In 1914, Joe Hill was arrested in Salt Lake City, Utah, and

The Great Rail strike of 1877 was one of the first violent conflicts between workers and employers.

charged with murder. Twenty-two months later, despite nationwide and international protests, he was executed by a firing squad. His body was taken to Chicago where over 30,000 people attended his funeral procession and eulogies were read in nine languages. The IWW opposed the participation of the United States in World War I and called for work stoppages in the midst of World War I. The federal government took legal action against IWW union leaders and by 1925 the union had disappeared.

The campaigns of the AFL to improve working conditions eventually resulted in the passage of laws prohibiting child labour, limiting the number of hours women could work, and establishing workers' compensation programmes for people who were injured on the job. The days of violent conflicts between workers and management came to an end. In 1935 a new union mainly for industrial workers was formed, the **Congress of Industrial Organizations** (**CIO**). The organization grew rapidly; by the late 1930s it had more members than the AFL, the union for skilled workers. AFL and the CIO merged in 1955 to form the **AFL/CIO** and this organisation today has about 14.5 million members. Like in Britain, the American unions are losing members, because industries which were union strongholds, such as the heavy industries, are on the decline. "**Blue-collar**" **workers** are being replaced by automation, and people working in the new service industries hesitate to join, especially in times of a prospering economy where inflation rates and unemployment figures are low. Even so, organized labor remains a strong force in the US economy and politics.

Sports

To say that Americans love sport would be an understatement – most of them are crazy about it. Going to a sporting event is a favourite pastime, and many Americans take their families for a day out to a stadium or a sports hall. Eating popcorn, hotdogs and ice-cream, drinking coke, watching the cheerleaders, enjoying the music of the brass band and, most important of all, cheering the home team makes for perfect entertainment. The sellers of food, drink and souvenirs at the stadiums do good business as well. Millions watch sports at home in front of their TV sets. The **Super Bowl game**, which is the championship final in US professional football, attracts the largest audience every year. Firms pay enormous sums to advertise during this broadcast. For other Americans sport is not only a source of entertainment and diversion from day-to-day worries, they practise it to keep fit. The number of runners and joggers has increased since the fitness craze swept the United States. In numerous health and fitness clubs people "work out", and hundreds of magazines, books and videos inform them how to do it properly and what equipment is needed. These examples illustrate the close connection between sport and business. Sport is a big money-maker today. Every year the thriving sports industry in the United States earns billions of dollars and employs thousands of people in the services and manufacturing sectors.

The recent history of the Olympic Games shows the close connection and interdependence of sport, television and industry. Until 1984 it was very difficult for the organiser of the games, the **International Olympic Committee (IOC)**, to find a country and a city which was willing and economically able to stage the Olympic games. Massive investments were needed to build the stadiums and the infrastructure to accommodate thousands of sportspeople from all over the world. More than once this task led to a financial disaster. Since the Olympic games of Los Angeles in 1984, however, this situation has changed completely. The Americans showed the world how to profit from the games through sponsorship. For the first time, multinational corporations (Kodak, IBM, AT&T, McDonald's) signed on as Official Sponsors who bought the rights to use the official Olympic emblem on their products and place advertising posters around the arenas and tracks. The fact that the Games attract a large viewing audience makes the Olympics an ideal platform for advertising. More than 3.2 billion people in 214 countries watched the Olympic Games in Atlanta, Georgia, in 1996. Commercial television stations need large audiences to sell their time to advertisers and consequently pay out huge amounts of money to secure the rights to broadcast the event. In 1995, America's **National Broadcasting Company** (**NBC**) paid $ 2.3 billion for exclusive US broadcast and cable TV rights to the 2004, 2006 and 2008 Summer and Winter Olympics, without even knowing where the games would take place. It is no wonder that today the International Olympic Committee is inundated with applications from cities all over the world competing heavily to be selected for the staging of the Games.

Most of the money which is earned in sport comes from television. Revenues from ticket sales alone cannot finance big sporting events. Such is the influence of the TV companies that sometimes the rules of the game or time tables are changed to allow for better TV coverage. In tennis the 'tiebreaker' was introduced to shorten televised matches, time-outs are used to show commercials, and most baseball matches take place at night, because this is the best time ('prime time') to reach a large audience. Several (industrial action) strikes which were staged in the past underline the fact that sport has turned into an industry. In 1981 the major League baseball players went on strike, in 1987 the players of the **National Football League** did the same, and in 1999 the basket ball players refused to play until their pay was raised. Organized labour and collective bargaining have become an integral part of professional sports. Professionals earn as much money as film stars and know very well that team owners, TV companies and advertisers depend on their performance. Critics may deplore the continuing commercialisation of sports but there is no turning back the clock.

In Europe, there are sports clubs which organize games and matches – in the US it is the high schools, colleges and universities. When a college or a university has outstanding players among its ranks it not only increases the prestige of the institution, it is also important for its financial situation. Colleges and universities have to find their own resources and good money can be earned with a first-class football or basketball team. As a result, many colleges have resorted to granting scholarships to athletes because of their skills as sportsmen and less because of their academic abilities. Critics ridicule this fact, saying that in the American system "scholarships are given to illiterate football players". The close connection between professional and college sport is also illustrated by the fact that many professional football and basketball teams pick promising younger players from high school or college teams. The selecting of young college players to include them into professional sides is called "drafting". The annual football draft is broadcast live on TV.

Apart from the economic side there are also social and political aspects connected with sport. Sometimes sport is used for political aims. At the 1968 Olympics in Mexico two black US medallists raised their fists, the Black Power salute, in protest against racial discrimination while the American national anthem was being played. During the Cold War both superpowers exploited the Olympics as a forum for political protest. In 1980 the United States led a boycott which included Germany and Japan of the Olympic Games in Moscow because the Soviet Union had invaded Afghanistan. In retaliation, the Soviet Union and 13 Communist nations withdrew their athletes from the 1984 Olympics in Los Angeles. Sport has also helped to climb in society. Many poor boys and girls, often from black families, have achieved social recognition and economic success because of their athletic excellence, thus realizing their American dream in the world of sport.

American Sports Inventions

The big sporting events, apart from the Olympic Games, which draw the largest crowds and with which TV stations achieve the highest ratings are sports which were invented in the United States.

American Football

The Europeans have soccer – or association football – the Americans have a different sort of football which is a mixture of rugby and soccer. American football was first played in US colleges in the mid-19th century, and the first rules were drawn up at Princeton College in 1867. The game, which is played between September and January, resembles rugby, but forward passing of the ball is permitted. The object of the teams – 11 players are allowed on the field for each team at any one time – is to score touchdowns, which means to move the ball across the opposite goal line. One or more defensive players of the opposing squad attempt to bring the ballcarrier down to the ground by tackling. Professional football is organised by the **National Football League** (founded in 1920), which consists of two groups, called conferences, the **American Football Conference** (**AFC**) and **National Football Conference** (**NFC**). At the end of each season the winners of the two conferences meet in a series of play-off games each January for the **Super Bowl** (instituted 1966–1967) to determine the national champion. An outstanding American football player was Walter Payton of the Chicago Bears – or 'Sweetness', as he came to be known – who gained more yards and scored more touchdowns than any other running back by the time he retired. Another hero of the game was Orenthal James Simpson, who came from San Francisco. He was nicknamed 'The Juice', because of his initials O. J. which also stand for 'orange juice'. In football he gained fame as one of the best and fastest running backs. Because of his outstanding qualities as a sprinter Simpson was at a time selected for a US 440-yard relay team which eventually set up a new world record. After his football career Simpson worked successfully as a sports commentator and appeared on television and in several films of the "Naked Gun" series. In 1995 Simpson was charged of killing his ex-wife and her friend. At the end of a sensational double murder trial which was televised worldwide Simpson was acquitted of the murder charges, but his popularity has since declined.

For millions, American football is the most exciting team sport. The game is played by elementary school, high school and college teams. The professional teams are organized in the National Football League and play for the championship in a game called the Super Bowl. The final is a great event and of national interest.

Baseball

Baseball is the national pastime in the USA. For Europeans it is probably the most puzzling sport – just like cricket or 'rounders', it has become an integral part of the American way of life and the most fascinating game. It is said that even Abraham Lincoln played baseball and was so fascinated by it that he kept a delegation of politicians waiting who had come to inform him of his nomination for the presidency until he had finished batting. At the beginning of the century a committee was set up to find out the origins of the sport and eventually came to the conclusion that Abner Doubleday, a West Point cadet, had invented baseball in 1839. However, these findings are doubtful, because there is evidence that the sport was played much earlier. Alexander Cartwright drew up the first rules in 1845. Baseball is played between April and October on a field which is laid out in the form of a square, called a diamond, by two sides of players with a bat and ball. Professional teams usually consist of 25 players. The aim of the game is to score as many runs as possible. A run is scored every time a player has made a complete circuit of the three bases and has returned to home plate. The visiting team goes up to bat first. The aim of the team in the field is to keep the batters from scoring by catching the ball. When a ball is hit out of the playing field, or if fielders cannot throw the runner out before he reaches home, the hit is good for four bases, or a home run.

The two major professional groups are the **American League** (14 teams) and the **National League** (16 teams), with each league having East, Central and West divisions. In addition to the major leagues there are minor leagues (classified as AAA, AA or A) in many American cities. The professional teams earn billions of dollars from ticket sales, the sales of food and drink, and television and marketing rights. Baseball players are regarded as the best paid professionals in the world of sport. At the end of a season the winners of the leagues determine in a best-of-seven games World Series the world champion. Famous teams include the **New York Yankees**, 23 times world champions, the **Chicago White Sox** and the **Toronto Blue Jays**, a Canadian team which won the World Series in 1992 and 1993. Baseball is becoming increasingly popular in Japan and Latin America. To honour Abner Doubleday and the heroes of the game the National Baseball Hall of Fame was dedicated in 1939 in Cooperstown, N.Y., where Doubleday had laid out his baseball field 100 years before. One of the first five players elected to the Baseball Hall of Fame was Babe Ruth (1895–1948). Ruth was born into a very poor family in Baltimore and became one of the most popular figures of professional baseball. He was the best left-handed pitcher in the American League and for a long time he held a record of 60 home runs in a season. Ruth played for the Boston Red Sox, the New York Yankees, the Boston Braves and at the height of his career Ruth was the highest paid player of his time: He received an annual salary of $80,000. In 1935 he played his last season and later became coach of the Brooklyn Dodgers. One of the best fielders of the New York Yankees was Joe DiMaggio (1914–1999), nicknamed Joltin' Joe and the Yankee Clipper, who holds the record for hitting safely in 56 consecutive games. His second wife was the film star Marilyn Monroe.

Baseball – "the Ball Game" – is a typically American sport which was invented in the first half of the 19th century.

Basketball

Basketball is a sport which is truly American in origin and has no European ancestors like American Football (a mixture of rugby and soccer) or baseball (England's cricket). Since its invention by James A. Naismith, a physical education instructor at the YMCA Training School in Springfield, Massachusetts, in 1891, it has always enjoyed great popularity. As a student Naismith played rugby, but he was put off by the rough side of it and thought about a new indoor ball game that would rule out physical contact. He chose elevated goals to minimize force on the ball and to keep some distance between the players and the actual scoring. As he could not find boxes to make the goals he used peach baskets. That is why the game became known as 'basketball' and not 'boxball', as the inventor had first intended to call it. The metal hoop was invented in 1906 and a bag of braided cord netting was attached to it. Today the game is practised by people all over the country on playgrounds and driveways. Although a few of the original principles of basketball have survived – offensive or defensive fouls are penalized to avoid physical contact – modern basketball has a wholly different look today. Five players make up a basketball team – a centre, two forwards, and two guards – and the aim of the game is to throw the ball through the opponent's basket, situated at the end of the court, and 10 ft (3.05 m) above the ground. Almost all professional basketball players are well over 6 ft (1.8 m) tall. The games are organized by the **National Basketball Association (NBA)**, which receives enormous sums from radio and TV stations for the rights to broadcast NBA games. The players also profit from the boom and basketball superstars earn more than a million dollars per year. The NBA formed a panel of experts to select the 50 greatest players in its history, without regard to position. Among them are legends such as Kareem Abdul-Jabbar, the inventor of the skyhook ('Hakenwurf'), Magic Johnson, famous for his no-look pass, and Michael 'Air' Jordan.

Kareem Abdul-Jabbar's original name was Lewis Ferdinand Alcindor, and he was born in New York City in 1947. In 1971 he adopted an Arabic name, which means "noble, powerful servant", when he converted from Catholicism to Islam. Scouts of the professional teams spotted him when he studied at the University of California. In 1969 he was selected by the Milwaukee Bucks in the NBA College Draft. In this annual draft the best college players are chosen by the professional NBA teams. The basic idea of the draft system is to provide a chance for the weaker teams to improve themselves, therefore the team with the worst record in the league is allowed to draft first. In 1985 the method was changed. Since then the teams that do not qualify for the play-offs enter a luck of the draw lottery, the winner of which has the first choice. Kareem was exceptionally tall (2.05 m) and he took advantage of his height to develop his signature shot, the 'skyhook'. He moved to the Los Angeles Lakers in 1984, and retired in 1989 with an exceptional list of achievements: No NBA player had ever scored more points, blocked more shots, won more **Most Valuable Player Awards**, played in more **All-Star Games** or performed at an older age.

Michael (Jeffrey) Jordan was born in Brooklyn in 1963. He played with the Chicago Bulls from 1984, leading the team to four world championships and was a member of the USA Olympic gold medal-winning team in 1984 and 1992, the "Dream team". Due to his remarkable fitness Jordan could jump higher than anybody else – a fact which earned him the nickname 'Air Jordan'. He left the game in 1999. Another basketball superstar was 'Magic' Johnson, who shocked the sports world in 1991, when he announced his immediate retirement from professional basketball because he was infected with the AIDS virus. Earvin Johnson was born in Michigan in 1959. He was drafted in the Los Angeles Lakers in 1979 when he played for his hometown Michigan State University. Johnson became famous for his blind passes (no-look-passes). The NBA's top 50 list also includes stars such as Charles Barkley, Jerry Lucas, Hakeem Olajuwon and Shaquille O'Neal.

American Sports Legends

Football, baseball and basketball are the most popular sports in the United States, but American athletes are in the world top class in many more disciplines as well. Americans love winners and sportsmen or sportswomen with singular merits are never forgotten. In boxing Muhammad Ali enjoyed the reputation of a living legend – decades after winning his gold medal at the 1960 Olympic Games in Rome. Ali, who was born as Cassius Clay, won three world heavyweight championships and was renowned for his unique style of fighting which distinguished him from all other heavyweight boxers. "He floated like a butterfly and stung like a bee", fans praised Ali enthusiastically. In swimming America's sports legends include Johnny Weissmuller (1904–1984) and Mark Spitz. Weissmuller, whose parents immigrated to the United States from Austria, participated in the 1924 and 1928 Olympic Games American and won five gold medals. After his sport career he became a movie actor and starred in several films as Tarzan. Mark Spitz (born 1950) won seven gold medals in all events in which he participated at the 1972 Olympics in Munich – two more than the previous record holder. Fans of track and field events will always remember Jesse Owens, Bob Beamon and Carl Lewis. Jesse

Owens (1913–1980) won four gold medals in track and field events at the Olympic Games of 1936 in Berlin, staged by Adolf Hitler's Nazi regime as a demonstration of the superiority of the Aryan, or white, race. This aim was seriously undermined when the African American athlete James Cleveland ('Jesse') Owens achieved his Olympic triumphs. Bob Beamon (born 1946) shot to fame with a single jump he took at the 1968 Summer Olympic Games in Mexico City. Aided by Mexico City's thin air, Beamon landed at 8.90 meters, setting up a record which stood until 1991. After the Olympic Games Beamon never jumped more than 8.20 meters because he was plagued by a hip injury and he retired before the 1972 Olympics. Carl Lewis (born 1961) – together with Al Oerter – is the only athlete to win four Olympic gold medals in the same track-and-field event. At the 1984 Summer Games in Los Angeles, he equalled Jesse Owens' feat of the 1936 Olympics in Berlin by winning gold medals in the long jump, 100 meters, 200 meters, and the 4 × 100 meter relay. When Lewis ended his Olympic career he had won nine gold and one silver medal altogether. The list of outstanding athletes is almost endless. Tennis supporters admire Bill Tilden (1893–1953), the first American tennis player to win the men's singles at Wimbledon in 1920, or Billie Jean King, Martina Navratilova, John McEnroe or Pete Sampras. For ice hockey fans Canadian Wayne Gretzky is the greatest player of all time, who ranks with basketball's Michael Jordan and soccer's Pele as one of the greatest athletes of the 20th century. Gretzky played for the Canadian team Edmonton Oilers – members of the American **National Hockey League** (NHL) since the 1979 to 1980 season –, and later in Los Angeles, St. Louis and New York. He scored more goals in a season than anybody else and in 1993 became the highest-paid player. When he retired in 1999, the NHL decided never to use his jersey number (99) again.

Americans live in a competitive society, and the world of sport is a reflection of it. Playing a game just for the fun of it is becoming a rarity. At the centre of sports which receive nationwide media coverage is competition. This desire to watch opponents combating to win in all kinds of sports is the reason for the great popularity and the commercialisation of sport today.

The USA – A World Power

Different Views of the United States

Hollywood, Mickey Mouse, McDonald's and Hemingway – ask anybody what he thinks about America and you will get hundreds of different answers. To many America is the "**land of promise, the land of the free**" – the dream land where the streets are paved with gold, the land of open opportunities: "From dishwasher to millionaire". This is the impression people have who live in poverty, in dictatorships, in countries of war and unrest, people who would like to get away from their homelands and make a fresh start in the New World. It is the America of the immigrants of the 19th century, of the Mexican illegal immigrants, the "wetbacks", the Vietnamese and Yugoslavian refugees of today. The underprivileged and dispossessed of the world still hang on to this view of the United States.

Hopeful Mexicans at the border between Texas and Mexico: one per cent of the US population are undocumented immigrants.

For others America is the "devil across the sea", the superpower which interferes in the inner affairs of countries around the world as soon as America's political or economic interests are endangered. It is the image of a nation which plays the policeman and acts in the name of liberty and democracy but which, in reality, pursues its own selfish interests. In some Asian and Middle East countries, the USA is regarded as a hostile imperial power and more than once, in times of crises, anti-American feelings erupt in violent attacks against US installations: Embassies are attacked or the American flag is burned. America is also seen as the country where violence and the use of guns has become widespread, where people are ruthlessly "hired and fired" from their jobs, where millions still live in poverty and have no social security. This is how the French historian André Kaspi explains the frequently negative view: "With the United States as the only source of world hegemony, and with American industrial and cultural influence so strong, there's a natural desire by other nations to assert their independence."

When the newly elected president of the United States is sworn in at the Inauguration ceremony he delivers a keynote speech in which he hardly ever misses to define America's role in world politics. Like most of his predecessors in the 20th century George W. Bush declared in his Inaugural Address of 2001 that America was determined to play its part as world leader and to exercise military power should the country's interests be affected. For many years America has traditionally considered itself as the guardian of freedom and justice around the world. This has not always been so. Since the beginnings of the nation, US foreign policy has passed through several stages which are connected with the names of the US presidents James Monroe, Theodore Roosevelt and Harry S. Truman.

America's Changing Role in the World

From Isolationism to Interventionism

The **Monroe Doctrine** (1823): For most of 19th century, the interests of the people of the United States were concentrated on their own affairs. All efforts were directed at the conquest of new territories, pushing the frontier further West. Americans were mainly concerned about the outcome of the **Civil War** (1861–1865). The fight between the South and the North over political influence, about the question of slavery and the future of the Union were of paramount importance. When the Civil War came to an end, the era of Reconstruction began. The main concern was to rebuild the Union politically and to promote the economic development of the country. The North had made emancipation, the freeing of all slaves, a war aim, and after the defeat of the Southern states the problem of how to secure the rights of the freed slaves as equal citizens arose. The wrecked plantation economy in the South had to be revived without the slavery system. The slaves, too, had to cope with their new situation. Many wanted to stay in the South, wandering around aimlessly, until they eventually returned to the plantations to take up work as tenants. Others headed North into the industrial areas of the US. All in all, Americans were fully occupied with their home affairs and were therefore not very interested in what was going on in Europe. That is why they kept to a principle of foreign policy which President James **Monroe** (1758–1831) had developed in his seventh annual address to the US Congress on December 2, 1823. The **doctrine** which bears his name became one of the foundations of US policy in the 19th century. In it James Monroe, the fifth president of the United States (1817–1825), declared that the interests of the US lay in the New World and in Latin America. At the same time he warned European nations against interfering in the affairs on the American continents.

The Monroe Doctrine became one of the foundations of US policy in the 19th century and can be regarded as the United States' first confident declaration of its importance in global affairs.

The **Roosevelt Doctrine** (1904): By the end of the 19th century the United States had finally recovered from the devastating effects of the Civil War. The Industrial Revolution was in full swing. New inventions and technologies brought about unprecedented economic growth and prosperity. The building of the railway helped the opening up of the Continent by providing a connection between East and West. New machinery made the American agriculture the most efficient in the world. After the settlement of the Far West new markets for American products were needed and the country began to reach out beyond its frontiers into Latin America and the Pacific: Feeling strong enough to claim status as world power, America gave up its "**splendid isolation**". The new way to look at America's role in the world was expressed by Theodore Roosevelt (1858–1919), who was to become the 26th president of the United States (1901–1909). Roosevelt believed America should play a major role in world affairs and exert more influence. As President he mediated an end to the Russo-Japanese war – a formidable achievement for which he was awarded the Nobel Peace Prize in 1906. Theodore Roosevelt's foreign policy centred on a belief that strong countries survive while weak ones perish. He saw in Germany the greatest threat to the US and supported the expansion of the US navy into a modern fleet. Roosevelt extended the Monroe Doctrine in 1904 by declaring that the US would prohibit any non-American intervention in Latin-American affairs. He also affirmed the right of the US to intervene in any country in the Latin American area which showed political unrest. Thus the United States, for the first time, took on the role as "**police power**". This policy became known as the **Roosevelt Doctrine**. An example of the new imperialist policy of the United States was the landing of American marines in Haiti (1915) to put an end to struggles between the blacks and the mulattoes and re-establish order on the island. The US occupied Haiti until 1934. The majority of Americans, however, still remained uninterested in foreign policy. This view changed when World War I broke out in Europe.

Democrat Theodore Roosevelt (1858–1919) was not only the youngest man ever to become President of the United States – at age 42 –, but also a gifted and powerful speaker.

The landing of US marines on Haiti in 1915, to put an end to killings of political prisoners, was seen as an imperialist invasion.

The **Truman Doctrine**: The United States hesitated to enter World War I and only after President Wilson's War Message to Congress did the mood in the country eventually change. This change was brought about by German submarine warfare and the sinking of the British vessels Lusitania (1915) and Sussex (1916). Both sinkings caused the loss of more than a hundred American lives, and when the Germans despite promises not to sink merchant vessels continued with their unrestricted submarine warfare, the Americans felt that the time to act had come. In 1917 the United States decided to join the allies in their fight against Germany. However, after the end of World War I and the signing of the **Treaty of Versailles** in 1919, the US withdrew again from Europe. Britain and France were disappointed that the Americans did not join the **League of Nations**, but wanted to return to their policy of isolationism in foreign politics once more.

The US was again late in entering World War II and only after an event which concerned American interests did the country decide to take up the fight. The United States tried for some time to stay clear of the continuing conflict between the British and French governments with Germany's Nazi regime. When World War II eventually broke out in 1939, US President F. D. Roosevelt supported the war effort of the British and French in various forms. It was the Japanese air attack on the American naval port of **Pearl Harbour** (Hawaii) in 1941 which catapulted the US into the war. The invasion of the American and British Forces on **D-Day**, June 6, 1944, in Normandy decided the war in favour of the Allies. On May 7, 1945, Germany surrendered and on August 8, 1945 the war in the Pacific came to an end after the dropping of two US atomic bombs on the Japanese cities of Hiroshima and Nagasaki. This time, however, the Americans acted differently in comparison to World War I, they did not turn their backs on European and world politics. On the contrary, from 1945 the United States assumed a strong leadership in world affairs. Politicians in Europe welcomed this change in the attitude of US foreign policy because they felt that a strong helping hand from the United States was needed in the re-construction of Europe and the emerging conflict with the Communist Eastern bloc. The US played a dominant role in the creation of the **United Nations Organisation** (**UNO**) and of the **North Atlantic Treaty Organisation** (**NATO**), the Western European Union defence group. The **US Marshall plan** was of vital importance for the rebuilding of devastated Germany.

The aim of the plan was not only to help the Germans recover from the Nazis and the Third Reich to make a fresh start, but also to a avoid a political and economic vacuum in Central Europe, which might then be filled by an expansionist Communist Soviet Union.

Policy of Containment

In 1946, shortly after the signing of the Potsdam agreement, animosities between the Western allies and the leader of the Soviet Union, Jossip Stalin, began to develop. Initially, there were political discrepancies about the control over defeated Germany and strategic differences about military arrangements in Greece and Turkey. The struggle eventually led to the formation of two bitterly opposed blocks: the United States with its Western European allies on one side and the USSR and Communist countries on the other. The US and its partners suspected that the Soviet Union wanted to extend its influence both in Eastern and Western Europe by installing Communist governments. In order to prevent Western Europe becoming Communist, the US government adopted a new strategy towards Russia, which was called **Policy of Containment**. This policy led to the outbreak of what the American journalist Herbert Swope in a 1947 speech called the **Cold War**.

McCarthyism in the 1950s: President Truman rejected McCarthy's charges that the Department of State employed Communists.

In the United States Senator Joseph R. McCarthy, a Republican from Wisconsin, created an atmosphere of anti-communist hysteria. By exploiting fears aroused by the Truman administration of a radical subversion of the American society McCarthy set out on a crusade to root out communism within the United States. A Committee on Un-American Activities investigated the lives and writings of many intellectuals and government officials. Most people who had to appear before the Committee could prove that they were innocent, but the lives of many were ruined.

During the Cold War the relationship between the Capitalist/Pro-American West and the Communist East was at freezing point. Eastern Europe was placed behind a military and political barrier known as the Iron Curtain. In the times of the Cold War several serious confrontations between the West and the East occurred and there were fears that a Third World War would erupt. Major confrontations were the building of the **Berlin Wall** (1961) and the **Cuba Crisis** (1962), when the Soviet Union wanted to install missiles on the doorstep of the United States, in Communist Cuba.

The **arms race** and the **race in space** must also be seen in the light of the fierce competition between the two superpowers. Both wanted to prove to the world the superiority of their political and economic systems. In 1957 the USSR had put a small aluminium satellite, 58 cm in diameter and weighing 84 kg, into orbit. The Russian success with Sputnik 1 caused a shock in the United States which was trailing behind in the development of rockets and satellites. The achievement of the Soviets was seen as a challenge and efforts were increased, which meant more money was made available, to form a US space programme. In 1960 President Kennedy committed the United States to landing a man on the Moon before 1970. As soon as the **Apollo Program** had succeeded, on July 20, 1969, in landing two astronauts on the moon, funds were reduced once again, because the free West had won the race in space.

The USA and Europe

America's Tarnished Image

In the first years after World War II the United States was seen as the liberator and the defender against Communism. However, gradually the image of the unselfish and unerring leader of the free West began to crumble and relations between the European allies and the United States cooled down. The Britons were the first to feel a certain amount of disappointment with their former war ally.

Many Britons were convinced that America used its power ruthlessly to bring about Britain's downfall as a leading world power by helping to dismantle the British Empire and replace it by American power. Britain felt left alone by the US in the Suez crisis. In 1956 the Egyptian President Nasser had seized the Suez Canal, which was to a large extent owned by British and French stockholders. When forces of Britain, France and Israel tried to occupy the canal zone, the United States did not support its European allies, perhaps for fear of a Soviet counter attack. Harold Macmillan, who was Conservative Prime Minister of Great Britain from 1957 to 1963, put it this way: "We are the Greeks in the new Roman Empire". The majority of British politicians believed that the United States was doing everything possible to weaken Britain's political status in the world.

President John F. Kennedy welcomes back two CIA agents who took part in the ill-fated landing at the Bay of Pigs in Cuba.

The trauma of the Vietnam War is not yet over: Many Americans still feel it was a big mistake to get involved.

In other European countries like France and Germany, the American image was being tarnished by the reluctance of the Americans to grant equal rights to their black countrymen and by military and political interventions which resulted from America's policy of containment. This strategy often narrowed the views of the country's political leaders and made them take decisions which, seen from today, must be judged as foreign policy blunders. Some of these mistakes were made during John F. Kennedy's presidency: the beginning of American involvement in Vietnam and the **Bay of Pigs** disaster. Because of Kennedy's untimely, violent death and the fact that the media turned him into a myth, his political errors were covered up for a long time. Only in recent years have historians started to paint a more realistic picture of Kennedy's political weaknesses. In April 1961 he ordered approximately 1,500 Cuban exiles, organized and financed by the **US Central Intelligence Agency** (**CIA**), to land on Cuba at the Bay of Pigs. Their mission was to overthrow the revolutionary regime of Fidel Castro, who in 1959 had turned Cuba into a Communist country. The operation was a complete failure. The invaders were captured and in the following trial in Havana the United States was exposed to the world as the mastermind of the plan driven by imperialist striving for power. Even more disastrous was Kennedy's decision to send US soldiers to the Far East to fight Communism in war-torn Vietnam.

The **Vietnam War**, which lasted from the mid-1950s until 1975, was the second war in Vietnam. In the First Indochina War Vietnamese nationalists had fought for independence from the French colonial regime. In the summer of 1954 France and Vietnam signed the **Geneva Peace Accords**, in which the temporary partition of Vietnam at the 17th line of latitude was laid down to allow France a face-saving defeat. It was also agreed that in 1956 Vietnam would hold national elections with which the temporary division of the nation would end. The United States, however, did not support the Geneva Accords because it was thought they granted too much power to the Communist Party of Vietnam. Consequently, when the regime in South Vietnam under Ngo Dinh Diem refused to hold the promised elections because they feared the popular nationalist Ho Chi Minh would win, the United States backed Diem's refusal. The result was an escalating conflict between the Republic of Vietnam in the South, and the Communist Democratic Republic of Vietnam in the North led by Ho Chi Minh. The revolutionary movement of the Vietcong took up the fight against Diem's regime on southern territory. The United States sent more and more combat troops to help Diem and started bombing military installations and cities in Northern Vietnam. The use of chemical weapons such as **Napalm bombs** (**Agent Orange**) had catastrophic effects on people and the landscape. The backing of the Saigon regime and the cruelty of the bombings tarnished the image of the United States and roused massive protests all over the world. On the streets of Saigon Buddhist monks killed themselves by setting fire to their bodies. The pictures of the monks engulfed in flames made world headlines. In Germany students took to the streets shouting the name of the leader of Communist North Vietnam, Ho Chi Minh, on their anti-American demonstrations. The Americans eventually had to admit their military power was ineffectual against the guerrilla tactics of the Vietcong. The Vietnam war, which President Kennedy and his successor President Johnson had meant to be "a limited war", ended with defeat. In 1975 a peace treaty was signed and Vietnam was formally reunified in 1976. The war, in the course of which the US air force had dropped three times as many bombs as during World War II, had devastated Indochina and claimed the lives of about 58,000 Americans and 2 to 3 million Indochinese. John F. Kennedy's misjudgement cost the United States over $ 150 billion, and it took the US economy several years to make up for the loss. However, the war in Indochina was not only a setback to the policy of containment in Asia, but more than anything else a shock to American self-confidence from which it has taken the nation much longer to recover. In films like "Apocalypse Now", "Platoon", "The Deer Hunter" and "The Killing Fields" the trauma of Vietnam is the central theme.

Unrest At Home

It was not only the Vietnam war which raised doubts about America's self-complacency. At home there were problems, too, which cast a shadow on the world defender of human rights, personal liberty and democratic government. The 1960s were years of unrest when the Civil Rights Movement, the struggle of the black Americans for equal rights, gathered momentum. In this fight they gained world-wide support and the US government came under heavy fire both at home and abroad. It was above all the younger generation that voiced its protest. In 1969, at a place called **Woodstock**, about 100 miles from New York, a crowd of 400,000 people came together to listen to singers and bands like Joan Baez, The Who, Jimi Hendrix, Joe Cocker, Jefferson Airplane and many others who sang for love and peace, against the Vietnam war and articulated the feelings of what came to be know as the **Hippie movement**. In Europe, too, young people in ever-increasing numbers demanded an end to the arms race between the USA and the USSR and the use of military force to achieve political aims. In England and Germany it became a tradition at Easter time to stage protest marches (**Aldermaston Campaign for Nuclear Disarmament**) when many activists called for a freeze on nuclear testing and disarmament. John Lennon wrote his song "Give peace a chance", and the slogan "**make love not war**" was coined.

The Era of Détente

By the 1970s the Cold War came to an end and the United States began to pursue a policy of **détente**. The Soviet Union agreed to take up talks on **disarmament** to put an end to the costly arms race, being deep in economic difficulties. Negotiations eventually led to two major agreements, SALT I and SALT II (**Strategic Arms Limitation Talks**), which provided for the limitation of defensive and offensive weapons. In spite of the SALT agreements the United States increased its defence spending again during Reagan's presidency in the 1980s. Millions of dollars went into **Strategic Defense Initiative (SDI)** programme, more commonly known as "**Star Wars**", a sort of military base in space. However, despite this setback arms control talks were resumed. Eventually the Communist empire in Eastern Europe disintegrated, when the **Warsaw Pact** collapsed and the Soviet Union dissolved. The era which was characterised by the conflict between Capitalism and Communism came to an end. Since then world power is no longer distributed between the two superpowers and the United States has been the only superpower and most influential world leader.

America's New Role

Since the disintegration of the Soviet Union and the collapse of the Communist bloc the United States has held a stronger position in world politics than ever before. President Clinton used America's new role as the only world leader to mediate in conflicts. He tried to conciliate between Palestinians and Israelis and he exerted his influence to promote a peace settlement between the conflicting parties in Northern Ireland. In several parts of the world American forces intervened. This time, however, together with soldiers from other countries under the auspices of the United Nations, in order to avoid the impression that America wanted to take advantage of its singular military and economic strength.

During the presidential election campaign of 2000 the two aspirants for the office of president, George W. Bush and Al Gore, were divided on many issues concerning home politics, e. g. the problem of social security or the **Medicare** program. However, there was next to no disagreement in the field of foreign policy. Both supported a world role for the United States. The Democrat candidate Al Gore spoke of the United States as a model for other nations, especially those struggling to build democracy. He viewed the United States as a country standing for human rights, which included taking action where possible to combat genocide and ethnic cleansing. The challenger Bush even supported the Clinton administration's efforts to achieve peace in the Middle East and also its policy toward Yugoslavia. Although he said the United States should not attempt to dictate policy to other countries he made it clear that he would send troops if it were in the nation's interests. For most Americans, Europe and the troubles on the Balkans or some other part of the world are far away. Therefore they question whether their government should spend so much money and risk the lives of American soldiers to keep peace in some remote country. Politicians in the US have taken up this widespread view and want their European partners to assume more responsibility as peacekeepers in the Balkans for example, so that US troops could be withdrawn. This is what is being said in public – however, no American president will today return to the Monroe Doctrine and concentrate the nation's interests on the American continent. The new President will make sure that not only the 20th but also the 21st century will be "an American Century", that the United States will keep its position as world leader.

Stichwortverzeichnis

Bildnachweis

Titelbild: © Corel Corporation 1997
S. 3, links: © Boston Athenæum
S. 3, rechts: © The Museum of Fine Arts, Boston
S. 5, links: © Metropolitan Museum of Fine Art
S. 5, Mitte: © Library of Congress
S. 5, rechts: © Charles Wilson Peale, Washington-Custis-Lee Collection, Washington and Lee University, Lexington, Virginia
S. 8: © Library of Congress
S. 16: © Thomas Felkner
S. 18: © Ullstein Bild
S. 22: © Thomas Felkner
S. 23: © The Norman Rockwell Family Trust
S. 28: Bill Pierce / Time Magazine © Intertopics
S. 31: © Library of Congress
S. 41, links: © dpa
S. 41, rechts: © Markus Kiechle
S. 42: © National Park Service Photos
S. 43: © National Park Service Photos
S. 44, links: © USIS
S. 44, rechts: © National Park Service Photos
S. 50, oben: © Crown Publishers
S. 50, unten: © Markus Kiechle
S. 56: © Library of Congress
S. 59, links: © Magnum, Eve Arnold
S. 59, rechts: © USIS
S. 63: © John Launois, Black Star
S. 72: © Markus Kiechle
S. 75: © Crown Publishers
S. 79: © Harald Steinhofer
S. 82: © Christine Rieger
S. 86: © Crown Publishers
S. 89: © Crown Publishers
S. 99: © Ford Archives
S. 102: © Chicago Tribune – New York News Syndicate Inc.
S. 108: © Crown Publishers

S. 110: © Picture Press
S. 113: © Library of Congress
S. 118: © Ford Motor Company
S. 120: © Library of Congress
S. 126: © Anuschka Krichbaum
S. 127: © Anuschka Krichbaum
S. 131: © Magnum, Alex Webb
S. 133: © Brown Brothers
S. 134: © Library of Congress
S. 135: © Ullstein Bild
S. 137, links: © AP-Photo
S. 137, rechts: © AP-Photo

Wir danken allen Rechteinhabern für die Abdruckgenehmigung.
Der Verlag war bemüht, die Urheber der abgedruckten Bilder ausfindig zu machen. Wo dies nicht gelungen ist, bitten wir diese, sich ggf. an den Verlag zu wenden.

Ihre Meinung ist uns wichtig!

Ihre Anregungen sind uns immer willkommen.
Bitte informieren Sie uns mit diesem Schein über Ihre Verbesserungsvorschläge!

Titel-Nr.	Seite	Fehler, Vorschlag

Bitte hier abtrennen

Damit lernen einfacher wird... **STARK**

10-V1T

Bitte ausfüllen und im frankierten Umschlag an uns einsenden. Für Fensterkuverts geeignet.

Zutreffendes bitte ankreuzen!

Die Absenderin/der Absender ist:

- ☐ Lehrer/in
- ☐ Fachbetreuer/in
  Fächer: ______
- ☐ Seminarlehrer/in
  Fächer: ______
- ☐ Regierungsfachberater/in
  Fächer: ______
- ☐ Oberstufenbetreuer/in
- ☐ Schulleiter/in
- ☐ Referendar/in, Termin 2. Staatsexamen: ______
- ☐ Leiter/in Lehrerbibliothek
- ☐ Leiter/in Schülerbibliothek
- ☐ Sekretariat
- ☐ Eltern
- ☐ Schüler/in, Klasse: ______
- ☐ Sonstiges: ______

Unterrichtsfächer: **(Bei Lehrkräften!)**

______

STARK Verlag
Postfach 1852
85318 Freising

Kennen Sie Ihre Kundennummer?
Bitte hier eintragen.

Absender **(Bitte in Druckbuchstaben!)**

Name/Vorname

Straße/Nr.

PLZ/Ort

Telefon privat für Rückfragen | **Geburtsjahr**

E-Mail-Adresse

Schule/Schulstempel **(Bitte immer angeben!)**

Bitte hier abtrennen

(Bitte blättern Sie um)

Natürlich führen wir noch mehr Buchtitel für alle Schularten. Wir informieren Sie gerne!

Telefon: 0 81 61/17 90 | **Internet: www.stark-verlag.de**

Telefax: 0 81 61/179-51 | **E-Mail: info@stark-verlag.de**

Deutsch

Grundlagen, Arbeitstechniken u. Methoden	Best.-Nr. 944062
Aufsatz Oberstufe	Best.-Nr. 84401
Abitur-Wissen Textinterpretation Lyrik, Drama, Epik	Best.-Nr. 944061
Abitur-Wissen Deutsche Literaturgeschichte gk/LK	Best.-Nr. 94405
Abitur-Wissen Deutsch Prüfungswissen Oberstufe gk/LK	Best.-Nr. 94400
Lexikon Autoren und Werke	Best.-Nr. 944081
Deutsch – Interpretationshilfen 1	Best.-Nr. 94407
Deutsch – Interpretationshilfen 2	Best.-Nr. 94408

Interpretationshilfen zu Einzellektüren:

Leben des Galilei	Best.-Nr. 2400011
Am kürzeren Ende der Sonnenallee	Best.-Nr. 2400201
Dantons Tod	Best.-Nr. 2400121
Aus dem Leben eines Taugenichts	Best.-Nr. 2400071
Das Marmorbild	Best.-Nr. 2400081
Homo faber	Best.-Nr. 2400031
Faust I	Best.-Nr. 2400511
Goethe *Gedichte (1771–1783)*	Best.-Nr. 2400181
Der fremde Freund/Drachenblut	Best.-Nr. 2400061
Die Verwandlung/Das Urteil	Best.-Nr. 2400141
Michael Kohlhaas	Best.-Nr. 2400111
Die folgende Geschichte	Best.-Nr. 2400251
Don Carlos	Best.-Nr. 2400161
Der Vorleser	Best.-Nr. 2400101
Schlafes Bruder	Best.-Nr. 2400021
Antigone	Best.-Nr. 2400221

Französisch/Latein

Textaufgaben zur Landeskunde Frankreich	Best.-Nr. 94501
Französisch – Wortschatz	Best.-Nr. 94503
Textaufgaben zur Literatur gk/LK	Best.-Nr. 94502
Französisch – Literaturgeschichte	Best.-Nr. 94506
Französisch – Textarbeit	Best.-Nr. 94504
Französisch – Wortschatzübung Oberstufe	Best.-Nr. 94505
Interpretationshilfen 1 Lyrik	Best.-Nr. 94507
Interpretationshilfen 2 Prosa	Best.-Nr. 94508
Interpretationshilfen 3 Drama	Best.-Nr. 94509
Lateinische Literaturgeschichte	Best.-Nr. 94602
Latein Kurzgrammatik	Best.-Nr. 94601
Latein Wortkunde	Best.-Nr. 94603

Ratgeber für Schüler

Richtig Lernen – Tipps und Lernstrategien für die Oberstufe	Best.-Nr. 10483
Referate und Facharbeiten für die Oberstufe	Best.-Nr. 10484

Englisch

Englisch – Übersetzungsübung	Best.-Nr. 82454
Englisch – Grammatikübung Oberstufe	Best.-Nr. 82452
Englisch – Wortschatzübung Oberstufe	Best.-Nr. 82451
Englisch – Grundfertigkeiten des Schreibens	Best.-Nr. 94466
Englisch – Textaufgaben zur Literatur	Best.-Nr. 94462
Englisch – Grundlagen der Textarbeit	Best.-Nr. 94464
Englisch – Literaturgeschichte	Best.-Nr. 94465
Englisch – Übertritt in die Oberstufe	Best.-Nr. 82453
Abitur-Wissen Landeskunde Großbritannien	Best.-Nr. 94461
Abitur-Wissen Landeskunde USA	Best.-Nr. 94463
Englisch – Interpretationshilfen 1	Best.-Nr. 82455
Englisch – Interpretationshilfen 2	Best.-Nr. 82456

Interpretationshilfen zu Einzellektüren:

Moon Palace	Best.-Nr. 2500031
Lord of the Flies	Best.-Nr. 2500051
Changing Places	Best.-Nr. 2500091
Educating Rita	Best.-Nr. 2500061
Macbeth	Best.-Nr. 2500011
Romeo and Juliet	Best.-Nr. 2500041
Huckleberry Finn	Best.-Nr. 2500021

Religion/Ethik

Katholische Religion 1 – gk	Best.-Nr. 84991
Katholische Religion 2 – gk	Best.-Nr. 84992
Evangelische Religion 1 – gk	Best.-Nr. 94971
Ethische Positionen in historischer Entwicklung – gk	Best.-Nr. 94951
Abitur-Wissen Ev. Religionslehre gk Der Mensch zwischen Gott und Welt	Best.-Nr. 94973
Abitur-Wissen Ev. Religionslehre gk – Die Verantwortung des Christen in der Welt	Best.-Nr. 94974
Abitur-Wissen Glaube und Naturwissenschaft	Best.-Nr. 94977
Abitur-Wissen Jesus Christus	Best.-Nr. 94978
Abitur-Wissen Die Frage nach dem Menschen	Best.-Nr. 94990
Abitur-Wissen Philosophische Ethik	Best.-Nr. 94952
Abitur-Wissen Freiheit und Determination	Best.-Nr. 94954
Abitur-Wissen Recht und Gerechtigkeit	Best.-Nr. 94955
Abitur-Wissen Religion u. Weltanschauungen	Best.-Nr. 94956

Kunst

Grundwissen Malerei – LK	Best.-Nr. 94961
Analyse und Interpretation – LK	Best.-Nr. 94962

Sport

Sport Bewegungslehre – LK	Best.-Nr. 94981
Sport Trainingslehre – LK	Best.-Nr. 94982

Bestellungen bitte direkt an:
Stark Verlag · Postfach 1852 · 85318 Freising

Damit lernen einfacher wird...

STARK